Land, Labour and Economic Discourse

Land, Labour and
Economic Discourse

Keith Tribe

Routledge & Kegan Paul
London, Henley and Boston

First published in 1978
by Routledge & Kegan Paul Ltd
39 Store Street,
London WC1E 7DD,
Broadway House,
Newtown Road,
Henley-on-Thames,
Oxon RG9 1EN and
9 Park Street,
Boston, Mass. 02108, USA
Set in Times by
Computacomp (UK) Ltd, Fort William, Scotland
and printed in Great Britain by
Lowe & Brydone Printers Ltd
Thetford, Norfolk

British Library Cataloguing in Publication Data

Tribe, Keith

Land, labour and economic discourse.
1. Economics − History
2. Agriculture − Economic aspects − History
I. Title
333.7'6'09   HB75   78−40715

ISBN 0 7100 0002 2
ISBN 0 7100 0003 0 Pbk

In memory of Maurice Dobb, 1900–76

Contents

Figures

These are all reproduced by permission of the University of London Library.

Jacket illustration courtesy of Cambridge University Library.

Preface

This book addresses itself to an investigation of the conditions of existence of a specific discursive form, economic discourse. It has a dual objective: first, to question the manner in which 'economic writing' has been organised into the unities and sub-unities of the history of economics; and second to reconsider the effects of epistemological evaluations of discourse that have developed with the introduction of criteria drawn from the history and philosophy of the sciences into accounts of economic theory and its 'origins'.

Some comments on this latter point are made in Chapter 1, directing itself to the way in which the work of Kuhn and Lakatos has been pressed into service in the revamping of a conventional historical approach to economic theory. It is possible here at the same time to argue against the function of rationalist conceptions of 'history' in constituting diverse texts into temporal economic unities. In doing so, however, a knowledge of the standard authorities in the history of economics (associated with names such as Cannan, Schumpeter, Meek, Hutcheson, O'Brien and Dobb) is presupposed. Where specific acknowledgment or criticism demands that reference be made, it is provided; but aside from this, it was felt that a registration of degrees of divergence and convergence would interfere with the course of the argument. It is hoped that the presentation that follows stands up for itself, not needing recourse to a critical barrage for the maintenance of coherence and unity.

Instead, the secondary function of the text is a critique of epistemological evaluations of discourse that are associated with the work stimulated by Louis Althusser. Here again, this critique lies between the lines, relying on positions cogently argued in Barry Hindess's *Philosophy and Methodology in the Social Sciences*. However, some consideration is given in Chapter 1 to the work of Gaston

Bachelard, whose work in the history and philosophy of the sciences is the foundation for Althusser's first reformulation of the relation between science and ideology. The purpose of such consideration is not however to re-appropriate Bachelard's work, but rather to indicate the limits of this work for the investigation of discursive formations. No attempt is subsequently made to rewrite the history of economics as the account of the emergence of a 'science' from its 'ideological' precursor. This form of writing, in relying on underlying continuities that relate these two entities, simply restores in a different form the teleology of the history it seeks to rewrite.

To clarify matters, it might be appropriate in this Preface to refer briefly to two recent attempts to account for the origin of economics via the classification of scientific and ideological forms. The first of these is Osier's lengthy introduction to the French translation of Hodgskin's *Labour Defended against the Claims of Capital.* Here it is argued that Hodgskin's critique of Classical Political Economy permits the question of the scientificity of this form to be assessed: for if it is a science, Hodgskin's criticism can only be incidental to it; while if it is 'something else', such criticism can possibly transform it (Osier, 1976, p. 14). Consequently, an examination of the work of Smith follows which investigates the novelty of the ideas put forward in *The Wealth of Nations,* and concludes that the essence of the economy that Smith outlines is not a system at all, but rather a philosophical anthropology of the subject, man (Osier, 1976, pp. 22, 26). Hodgskin's critique, from the 'point of view of the working class' (p. 56), corrects the anthropological bias of political economy, and expresses the real relations of capitalism that political economy had fetishised (p. 73). What is notable about this treatment is that the unities that can be found in the textbooks of economics are simply taken over and reworked into a classification which carves up discourse into two sections, one of which is positive and the other of which is negative. Futhermore, this account of Classical Political Economy depends on a grid reading in which it is Marx's *Theories of Surplus Value* that provides the end-point and measure of the teleological history that is constructed. The economists of the late eighteenth and early nineteenth centuries are constructed as predecessors of Marx in which it is only the discourse of Marx that provides the rationality for judging their statements.

Hodgskin's theoretical basis for his critique is identified as his class position, and Osier elsewhere expresses this epistemological view whereby the utterances of human agents are constitutive of the status of discursive forms. This conception is elaborated in Therborn's *Science,*

Class and Society, especially in his chapter entitled 'The Economy and Economics of Capitalism'. Therborn (1976, p. 77) contends that 'economic discourse emerged as a concomitant of the rise of what this discourse was about: the capitalist economy', and proceeds to realise this conception of the relation between economy and economic theory in an account of the class positions of the foremost economists of the nineteenth century. For Therborn, the work of such writers is stamped with its origin in the bourgeoisie, a class which by virtue of its position is denied insight into the hidden workings of the capitalist economy. Marx, by adopting a proletarian standpoint, changes his position and gains access to this hidden inner core, consequently creating the first scientific analysis of capitalism.

For both Osier and Therborn, Classical Political Economy is indelibly stamped with the mark of its origin, an ideology of the bourgeoisie and thus an eternally failed knowledge, our interest in this carcase being maintained only for so long as the time it takes to establish the irrevocability of its fate. This practice not only prevents serious analysis of discursive forms, whereby (in this case) Marx's analysis of capitalist relations is scientific and therefore functions discursively as truth, Smith performing the role of a negative to this truth; more generally, such a representational epistemology restores the conditions of the philosophical reflection that Bachelard set out to reject. The categories of 'ideology' and 'science' therefore find no place in the chapters that follow.

This book is not intended to provide a 'history' of economic discourse, and the arrangement of the material that it presents is intended to reflect this. The fact that this material is apparently 'historical' – drawn from a past and organised into a loose chronology – should not be permitted to obscure the argument that the conditions of formation of economic discourse are not themselves temporal. No predecessors are constructed for Classical Political Economy; instead a series of arguments are advanced which attempt to undermine the coherence of the predecessors that have been written into the histories. The organisation of the chapters is dictated by a discussion of the possibilities of 'land' and 'labour' as economic categories. For there is no immanence in these two apparently essential terms of economic life which designates the discourses in which they emerge as 'economic discourses'. To demonstrate this a series of arguments are advanced, proposing that the category of 'rent' is a variant one related to either land or labour, that the notion of 'household' dominates conceptualisation of economic life in the seventeenth and eighteenth centuries, and that the incorporation of conceptions of land and labour into the treatises of agricultural production of the seventeenth and eighteenth centuries carries no necessary consequences for the form of analysis in which they are implicated. Finley (1970, p. 22) has proposed that this model of the household economy dominates 'economics' until the eighteenth century, and the texts which take their place within this form cannot therefore be constituted as precursors of Classical Economics. The argument of the later chapters seeks to emphasise that the fact of chronological precedence cannot be converted into a condition of existence for a discourse which appears to share some common ground with earlier discursive forms. An account of economic discourse cannot be related as a discursive genesis, nor as non-discursive emergence. The process of formation of economic discourse as a systematic exploration of forms of distribution and production between economic agents must be written in a manner which does not depend for its validity on the invocation of a chronology, nor on the privilege of a materially effective and unconditioned economy. The purpose of this book is an attempt to explore this possibility.

All translations from original foreign-language material are mine.

I would like to express my gratitude to Liz Brown, Terry Counihan and Jim Tully, all of whom in various ways assisted in my work on this book. It is customary in such expressions of thanks to disassociate such friends from the awesome deficiencies in the work to hand, deficiencies which are piously ascribed to the hand of the author. Such pleading would be inappropriate here, for reasons that will I hope become obvious. There is a similarity between the idea that a wife is answerable to her husband and the notion that a text is the responsibility of its author. In both cases legal, economic and moral questions become fatally entwined. It is perhaps too much to hope that the conditions for the emancipation of women from men will also make possible the emancipation of texts from authors.

1

History and Discourse

This book investigates the manner in which, at the beginning of the nineteenth century, a novel discursive formation came into being, one whose structure is constituted by a specific conjunction of concepts of capital, profit, exchange, production and distribution. This event marks the birth of economic discourse.

But of course this has all been said before – most of the histories of economic theory assert that some similar event happened around this time, although if we turn to them we will in fact find an actual date given for this momentous occasion: 1776, the date of publication of Smith's *Wealth of Nations*. Quite naturally, any such birth is conditional on conception and gestation, a process which in this case occurs in the thoughts and early writings of Adam Smith. Then again no child comes into the world without assuming at once a set of forebears or predecessors, and simultaneously offering the potentiality of being in turn the predecessor of its own descendants. Thus the history of economics discovers its scope, object and method, and can proceed to constitute pre-histories and histories of a discourse that reflects eternally on the conditions of material existence of humanity – economics.

This 'economy' has always existed, while the theory which expresses its organisation only takes shape with the systematisation of the dispersed ideas which express it. A history of economics has therefore to articulate the unity of this dispersion and account for the development of the constituted discourse. But two questions can be posed to this rationalist project: first, what is the history of economics a history of? And second, what is historical about the histories that are produced in these writings? Set against the obviousness of what has been said above, the relevance of these questions seems dubious. But it is in fact the very naturalism of the forms of constituting such histories, referring us to events which have a pre-given beginning like a birth, publication of a book, and so on, that suppresses the theoretical bases on which they exist. And indeed, perhaps there is only one substantial divergence so far from the form of periodisation of economic discourse that the history of economics offers us – the historians state that economics proper begins in 1776, whereas the first paragraph of this chapter states that the date is in the early nineteenth century. But the divergence does run deeper than the customary scholastic debate over times and places, for it will be seen below that the history of economics 'creates' in 1776 modern 'economic theory' while that which arises in the nineteenth century is economic discourse. These two terms are not the same; and therefore 'economic discourse' is not here a synonym for that other unity of the histories, 'Classical Political Economy'. The nature and conditions of existence of this economic discourse is a problem to be investigated, a problem which can never be posed in the histories of economics.

The purpose of this introductory chapter is to show why this rash statement has some substance, and it consequently engages obliquely with a series of secondary texts which discuss the work of authors such as Smith, Hume, Ricardo, Mill and other more obscure figures. The subsequent chapters will in general refer only in passing to this literature of commentary, since a critical assessment of the various historical writings can only be a preliminary task in the examination of the texts of the economic archive, and can in no way substitute for it.

If we turn to some general histories of economics, it will be found that two competing starting-points for economics are cited, for in addition to Smith and his book we have the work of the Physiocrats, or more precisely Quesnay's *Tableau Economique*. However, these alternative origins are nominated in different fashions, for the latter is primarily selected for the apparent systematicity of the analytical project, while the actual nature of this project is never properly investigated. For example, Eagly (1974, p. 3) is seen to transform the *Tableau* into a capital input–commodity output matrix in order to retain Quesnay as the originator of modern economic analysis; in this way the project of the Physiocrats is not only ignored, but positively transformed in the bland assumption that the 'annual advances' are what we would today call 'capital'. In general this mode of transformation is necessary to appropriate Physiocracy as the historical origin of economic analysis.

It is more usual, however, to nominate Smith as the originator of modern economics, since he was, as Barber says (1967, p. 27), 'concerned with developing a theory of economic growth'. *The Wealth of Nations* does not present the kind of expository rigour of the *Tableau*, and, as we will see later, only the first two Books of this lengthy work are usually dealt with in the histories.[1] And in addition this book is the only economic work that Smith published, conveniently removing the difficulty of establishing principles of evaluation for a set of contradictory texts by the same author; 1776, then, in a very real sense heralds the birth of economics. The prior existence of the author opens the possibility of investigating the genesis of this event, and indeed there have been some interesting discoveries of early lecture notes which facilitate the reconstruction of this genesis, and enable arguments to be settled concerning the incidence of various influences on the author – whether these be philosophical, literary or environmental.[2]

The principal reason, however, for the canonisation of Smith as the founder of modern economics is that *The Wealth of Nations* (Books I and II) is peculiarly susceptible to the imposition of a neo-classical grid; for the primary device which the history of economics employs for the demarcation of the economic archive is the structure of contemporary economic theory. A simple teleology makes possible the construction of a history of economics as the process of rational growth of the analysis of the economy. As Bachelard (1965, pp 24–7) argued, each science reworks its history as a history of its progress, producing a double recurrent history: a sanctioned history of the positive acts producing the knowledge, and a continually augmented peripheral history constituted by the elements that are discarded in the progress of the science. As an example of the more extreme and consciously recurrent texts on the history of economics, Blaug's *Economic Theory in Retrospect* (1968, p. 6) locates 'market exchange' as the central element of such a history and Adam Smith as its first theorist. Or again, one has only to turn to the book of essays published to mark the bicentenary of Smith's book to find the use of modern theory to stitch bits of *The Wealth of Nations* together as a contribution to international trade theory, price theory, and a whole series of entirely anachronistic phenomena (Skinner and Wilson, 1975). In the repetition of 'Adam Smith and ...' that is to be found on the contents page rests the form of appropriation of the past that characterises the history of economics.

There is of course a more obscure peripheral history that lurks in monographs and journals, a record of 'forgotten men', cast aside in the teleological advance of the sanctioned history. By using a specifically Keynesian grid Gordon is able to identify five such 'forgotten men' in the early nineteenth century who can be accounted for in the language of Keynesian economics. When these authors present components that are not compliant with such demands, such features are described as 'lapses' (Gordon, 1967, esp. pp. 5–6).[3] Or, on the other hand, Johnson's

Predecessors of Adam Smith constitutes a unified series of texts on the basis that the works of Hales, Malynes, Misselden, Mun and the rest can be compared with the work of Smith, although the procedure of comparison in each case inevitably constitutes the texts as deficient. The series of intellectual biographies that Johnson presents is thereby endowed with a unity of absence, for none of them can effectively realise that to which they merely contribute.[4]

The naturalisation of the problem of demarcation and periodisation via reference to the life of an author, his milieu and his acquaintances continually removes a questioning of the basis of the history on grounds other than those played out in the intellectual life of a mortal human being. But there is another possibility for a chronology, one which goes beyond the sporadic and fleeting existence of 'economic thinkers': the nature and development of the economy and society in which these authors live. It seems perfectly natural that attempts to provide a theory of the functioning of the economy should be conditional on the form and pace of development of the economy that provides a niche for the author. Further, reference to the economy provides a self-regulating form of demarcation and periodisation – for example, we can look into the late seventeenth and eighteenth centuries for economic theories of trade and money, since we know from economic histories that these things were central to these economies. The rise of manufacturing as a significant factor in the life of the nation thus suggests that a new form of theory will arise to supplant the so-called 'Mercantilist' theories. We need look no further than Roll's *History of Economic Thought* (1954, pp. 92ff.) to find such an argument put forward. But even here, where mercantile capital produces Mercantilism and manufacturing produces Classical Political Economy, it is necessary to realise this process through the mediation of an experiencing author who can translate these economic conditions into the discursive realm. In this way, the economy is presented as prior to or independent of its discursive characterisations and the latter conceived of as an adequate or inadequate reflection of it. But how can this economy be presented as independent of discursive characterisation and thus given privileged status as a measure of the discourse(s) that succeed or fail to reflect it? Only on condition that some dubious metaphysical distinction is made between the 'real world' and the 'world of ideas'. However, a sleight of hand intervenes whenever this form of distinction is invoked, for it is not in fact 'the economy' which governs the periodisation of 'economic thought' but a certain description of it, a particular discursive form. The pretended privilege of the real world over the world of ideas is nothing more than the privilege of one discursive order over another in which unconditioned descriptive statements condition theoretical ones; since the confrontation takes place within discourse, it cannot be anything else.

What is particularly insidious about this procedure is that it is assumed that since the economy is 'real' and 'material', mere reference to the texts of economic histories is sufficient for the character of the economy in question to be established. Nothing is therefore easier than to account for the rise of economic theory as the reflection of the first industrial revolution, the temporal and geographical coincidence of the two assuring the rectitude of the procedure. Unfortunately the basis on which the histories of this revolution are constructed are themselves teleological, casting the image of the process of formation of different modes of commodity production and circulation as one of technical development. In modern terms, the industrial revolution creates a new sector of the economy by changes in technique which combine to hegemonise the economy as a whole. The cotton industry is the classical locus of these technical developments, which are dated from 1760 with the spinning jenny, the first in a series of machines that were to transform textile fabrication from manufacturing to factory production. While it is not appropriate here to embark on a substantial revisionist critique of the historiography of the industrial revolution, some remarks must be made concerning the nature of the economic order which is referred to almost in passing in much of the literature, but which nevertheless plays a crucial part in the discussion of the explanatory value of economic theory.

By its very name, the 'industrial revolution' is proposed as a change in forms of production in the industrial sphere, and the primary change that is usually remarked on is the organisation of factory production based on machine processes using steampower sources.[5] Certain important factors are related to this: the invention of the appropriate machinery, the accumulation of the capital resources for the programmes of investment required, the creation of a labour force adequate to these new methods, and the construction of the factories within which these processes could be carried on. However, recent research has begun to provide the material for this long-established 'history' to be considered as either one-sided or in certain cases entirely misguided. The conception of the industrial revolution as a period of rapid technical advance requiring substantial inputs of money-capital is being displaced from its heroic pose and is being rewritten as a period of concentration and organisation of second- and third-hand equipment set to work in disused buildings and in fact requiring somewhat less disposable capital than preceding forms of production in which the materials' stock of the manufacturer, proceeding slowly through a dispersed and disorganised production process, represented a large portion of his assets. If there is such an occurrence that can be called an 'industrial revolution', then it is one characterised by a series of reorganisations of the production process, events whose significance was not always apparent to their contemporaries, and which have only recently become clearer to historians.

The early machinery of the industrial revolution was crude and basic, requiring more expenditure on maintenance than purchase, which could in any case have been acquired at the auction of a bankrupt's stock. In the late eighteenth century the most capital intensive of all industrial processes, textile manufacturing, was several times eclipsed in any one year's expenditure on capital formation by the money spent on shoeing horses (Crouzet, 1972, p. 22). The 'mills' were old barns or other buildings that were not designed specifically as factories, and given the available means of production control there was no advantage in large-scale enterprise (Heaton, 1972, pp. 86–7). Water power, rather than steam power, was the predominant source of energy, and when in the late eighteenth century all the best sites for water-mills in Oldham had been occupied, the new enterprises turned to horses, not steam, for their power (Cardwell, 1972, p. 85). The principal historians of industrial technology have stressed the low level of total steam horse-power before 1800, and the small scale of the machines then in use compared to the power of some of the water-wheels (Musson and Robinson, 1969, p. 72).

The shift from manufacture (in which the production process is based on handwork skills, even if extremely specialised, subdivided and either dispersed in the homes of the workmen or concentrated in a central manufactory) to factory production, in which the pace and organisation of production shifts into the control of the capitalist, is the central feature of the industrial economy at the end of the eighteenth century. It is not so much changes in technique, but changes in organisation that make the crucial difference. Machinery is not an index of modernity but rather is introduced to increase the control of the capitalist over the pace and flow of work. Some advanced capitalist enterprises could not in any case mechanise their basic processes, but this did not mean that they were thereby handicapped. For example, Wedgwood designed his pottery works at Etruria not around some set of machinery (which could not in any case be utilised in the pottery industry) but rather around a spatial flow of production: materials offloaded from the canal travelled through the factory from process to process in a semi-circle until they arrived back at the canal ready for shipment (McKendrick, 1961, p. 32). Chapman (1974, p. 470), in a survey of the organisation of eighteenth-century textile factories, has also concluded that the principal feature of the factory was the inauguration of flow production, which might or might not utilise new machinery for its execution.

The elements which entered into this reorganisation of production were various: the creation and disciplining of a skilled labour force (McKendrick, 1961); the development of new forms of accounting (Pollard, 1965); the standardisation of product quality; the utilisation of forms of credit and the emergence of new agencies able to advance such credit; the formation of a class of clerical workers and managers to administer the growing complexities of production and sales; and so on. The emergence of these features was only partial and hesitant at the end of the eighteenth century, and many of the elements that are assumed to be fully developed in the eighteenth century in fact only became fully developed perhaps a century later.

The concentration on machinery as the principal feature of the industrial revolution derives from the broad division of the economy into industrial and pre-industrial phases, a division which is buttressed by other questionable synonyms such as the market–non-market distinction and the traditional–modern dichotomy. These forms of demarcation resort to a technicism in their account of the movement from one to the other, in which the tangible presence of new machines and sources of energy are the representatives of the new order. This very tangibility suggests the idea that the contemporaries of these inventions could not but be aware of their existence and implications. And in this way the 'industrial revolution' becomes the backdrop to, and the necessary condition for, the development of economic theory.

We can take as an example the arguments which have surrounded the person and writings of Adam Smith, a man who lived for a time in the commercial city of Glasgow, and who was acquainted with many of the prominent industrial entrepreneurs of his time.[6] Hollander in his *Economics of Adam Smith* suggests that we can find in *The Wealth of Nations* a discussion of the economies of scale in factory processes, represented in the notion of 'division of labour':

It need only be added that while Smith's illustrations of division of labour were derived from relatively small-scale nail-making and pin-making plants he was aware of the large-scale iron works at Carron where there had 'lately been a considerable rise in the demand for labour'. Indeed, as we shall see, Smith entered into a highly sophisticated analysis of the effect of scale of *industry* upon the degree of division of labour practised at the plant. This in itself is eloquent testimonial to the fact that factory organisation was to Smith's mind well established and calling for detailed analysis.

Hollander assumes that the term 'division of labour' derives its explanatory force from its correspondence with the conditions prevailing in contemporary production processes. The term is therefore deployed as a means of assessing the modes of organisation of these processes present in the advanced factories of Smith's day. For Hollander, it matters little that the example that Smith uses in Book I of *The Wealth of Nations*, the celebrated pin factory, refers to a manufacturing enterprise and was in fact taken from the 'Épingles' article in the French *Encyclopédie* of 1755; the principle of subdivision of work remains the same. But even if we allow that this reference to production forms is a necessary element in a discursive proof, it must be stressed that the function of this 'division of labour' is quite distinct in manufacture and factories. In manufacture, the division of production into a series of discrete hand operations is simply a device for the rationalisation of these hand operations. In factory production, on the other hand, where the capitalist seeks to control the production process in order to better regulate it, the division of labour and the demarcation of skills is deployed according to principles of organisation of the production process to this end. As has been remarked above, the picture of 'division of labour' and 'economies of scale' that Hollander conjures up does not belong to the eighteenth century because in the prevailing conditions size meant chaos (cf. Pollard, 1965, ch. 2). Economies of scale can only emerge with the techniques that facilitate the organisation of a large volume of diverse operations in production, management and distribution. They are not inherent in industrial production itself, nor simply in the presence of a technical division of labour; in capitalist industrial production the division of processes is not based in the rational division of skills and the product, but rather in the exigencies of the organisation of the process of production as a whole.[7]

Another consequence of the manner in which the industrial order is summoned up as an explanatory device for the evaluation of a discursive form is that agricultural production cannot ever appear as a significant element, being characterised in the eighteenth century neither by division of labour nor by extensive use of machinery in production. This is despite the fact that agriculture was the dominant sphere of the economy at this time, and also the most intensively capitalist of any sector. Part of the reason for the neglect of agrarian capitalism in the attempts to account for the rise of economic discourse is that the economic histories that are available tend to focus on technical changes and the prevalence of small units of production. This disguises or evades the way in which the problems that agriculture faced at the end of the eighteenth century were problems in the organisation of capitalist enterprises, such as the calculation of input costs, the effective organisation of the production process and the selection of crops for production by reference to regional and national markets.[8] While it cannot of course be argued that agrarian production is a 'better' unconditioned referent for economic discourse than industrial production, it will be shown later that the constructs of the Classical Economists presupposed a one-product-commodity economy, which when cast in this light can be shown to have little or no relation to the organisation of production and distribution of industrial commodities. The distinction that will be made does not rest on the contrast between the artificiality of industrial processes and the naturalness of agricultural production, nor on the different sites on which they occur: the differences between industrial and agrarian economies are established in the form and time of commodity production, and the manner in which the circulation of the products affects calculations concerning production.

These comments concerning the 'industrial revolution' serve merely to underline the manner in which the reference to the development of an economy to explain the form of development of a discursive order results in a mis-specification of both. Not only is the economy 'different' from the conventional representations of it, and therefore the arguments made with its support are invalid; but the whole process of referring a discursive order to a non-discursive one for principles of validation is misconceived. And in any case, as was suggested above, the apparent movement from the non-discursive to the discursive in the process of a proof merely invokes the unconditioned privilege of one discourse over another.

However, it is not suggested that many historians of economics place decisive weight on such a procedure; the contemporary economy is instead deployed in the histories as a means of prior demarcation and periodisation, the substance of the narrative usually being devoted to the analysis of the works of authors and their decoding. In this process the interplay of authors and theories provides the material for the history, tracing the times and places of formation of new ideas, attributing them to this or that author, and investigating the process of mutual influence in the descent of a set of ideas over time. Such procedures have in recent years become more and more unsatisfactory, and historians have cast around for a framework which can provide some form of organisation in their accounts of the progress of economic theory. The principal area from which they have derived ideas has been the history of science, which has since the 1960s apparently been shaken by at least two major innovations in historiography, represented by the work of Kuhn and Lakatos.

Kuhn's *Structure of Scientific Revolutions* has, since its original publication in 1962, been the object of much interest in the social sciences, largely because of the manner in which it could be utilised in evaluations of the 'scientific' status of disciplines like sociology and psychology. For the historian of economics, terms like 'paradigm', 'scientific community' and 'revolution' offered the possibility of rewriting the history of economics as a science which progressed and developed in a fashion similar to the other sciences. The citation of Kuhn, considered at first daringly novel, has since then become almost mandatory, until the underpinning of whole texts involved a tacit consent to the Kuhnian historiography (Black, Coats and Goodwin, 1973). By the early 1970s, however, some doubt was being expressed concerning the effectiveness of constant reference to Kuhn in the construction of viable histories (Bronfenbrenner, 1970; Kunin and Weaver, 1971).[9] It was too easy, for example, to translate categories like Schumpeter's 'classical situation' into 'paradigm' and assume that this operation in some way clarified the issues involved (Stark, 1959). Or again, this translation of the Keynesian 'revolution' into the new terminology is simply one of many similar cases that abound in the literature (D. F. Gordon, 1965, pp. 123–4):

> Smith's postulate of the maximizing individual in a relatively free market and the successful application of this postulate to a wide variety of specific questions is our basic paradigm. It created a 'coherent scientific tradition' (most notably including Marx) and its presence can be seen by skimming the most current periodicals. Presumably the addition of the principle of variable factor proportions, or the notion of the consumer with relatively stable transitive preferences, is 'further articulation'. Its 'specification under new ... conditions' which constitutes 'normal research' can be indefinitely illustrated by analyses of monopoly and competition, tariffs and free trade, money and government deficits, excise and

income taxes, unions and minimum wage legislation – the list is long and well known.

In fact it can be argued that the problem here lies not with the economists but with the ideas advanced by Kuhn, for it has become clear that the initially appealing framework is not capable of doing the work that it is called upon to perform, as can be shown by a brief outline of *The Structure of Scientific Revolutions*.[10]

Kuhn introduced a model of the history of science based on periods of stability punctuated with spasmodic outbreaks of crisis and shift in the scientific enterprise. 'Paradigm' was the name given to the unity characteristic of the stable progress of 'normal science'; and it was with the emergence of anomalies within these paradigms that a period of crisis developed, a crisis which if not resolved or suppressed led to a period of 'extraordinary research' potentially overthrowing the old paradigm. This generally attractive and catastrophic schema had the air of authenticity, describing the way in which competition within the sciences took place and the possibility of a progressive development entirely changing the basis on which the science was organised. However, a problem arose whenever the paradigm for any science was isolated, since Kuhn relied on social criteria, expressed by the existence of communities of scientists, to provide a theoretical unity to the scientific paradigm, which was a clearly unsatisfactory state of affairs. A paradigm was thereby constituted by invoking a set of constituting subjects, and in the practical cases studied this resulted in sociological categories being called upon to perform epistemological distinctions. Furthermore, Kuhn could not distinguish between the formation of a paradigm and the shift from one paradigm to another, which is one of the crucial issues in the history of any science. The outcome of this and a whole series of related problems was that although there was a certain initial appeal in Kuhn's ideas for those seeking a way out of the more intractable difficulties of the history of economics, the actual introduction of the new terminology simply retranslated and compounded them. An example would be that the failure to specify any mechanics for the paradigm change led to a re-emergence of the simple chronology as the dominant instrument of these histories, whereby the succession of writers and texts is organised by reference to a calendar, rather than to the nature of the discursive forms themselves.

The arguments and proposals for the history of the sciences presented in *Structure of Scientific Revolutions* are of no use in considering the problems faced by the history of economics. However, it is significant that historians have looked to this kind of material for ideas, rather than to more traditional Anglo-American philosophical work, since a consequence has been to direct attention to *structure* and *discontinuity* in the construction of histories. While Kuhn's work in itself provided no solution to problems that it only partially posed, reference to such a body of work opened the way for discussions of method that had previously been absent from the history of economics. And the disillusion with Kuhn led not to a rejection of history and philosophy of science, but instead to a search for an alternative. One such alternative was found in the work of Imre Lakatos.

The methodology of scientific research programmes that Lakatos presents is a variant of a sophisticated Popperianism, and like Popper he has concentrated on the problems in attempting to provide criteria of demarcation between the sciences and metaphysics. Whereas Popper (1969, pp. 32–3) concentrates on individual propositions and statements that are then subjected to various tests to determine their falsifiability, Lakatos considers whole clusters of propositions that he calls 'research programmes'. Instead of being falsifiable in a simple fashion, these are constructed in a bipartite manner, such that only certain propositions are subjected to critical examination; and the structure also is subject only to retrospective judgment, for it is only after the event that it is possible to decide whether a given programme is progressing or degenerating.

The most complete outline of this methodology is to be found in Lakatos's contribution (1970) to the conference which was staged to discuss Kuhn's book. Here we find a distinction made between the 'core' of a programme and its protective belt of auxiliary theories that is permitted to be tested. Lakatos (1970, pp. 126–7) describes the process of testing as follows:

> Thus we do not eliminate a (syntactically) metaphysical theory if it clashes with a well-corroborated scientific theory, as naive falsificationism suggests. We eliminate it if it produces a degenerating shift in the long run and there is a better, rival, metaphysics to replace it. The methodology of a research programme with a 'metaphysical' core does not differ from one with a 'refutable' core except for the logical level of the inconsistencies which are the driving force of the programme.

The programme consists of methodological rules, some of them indicating paths of research to be avoided (the negative heuristic), others the paths that should be pursued (the positive heuristic). Every step in the development of the programme should be 'content-increasing', and this is ultimately the criterion for the assessment of the programme against its rivals. However, this assessment cannot take the form of a simple summing of anomalies in each case, for the positive heuristic prevents this. In addition, research programmes in the process of construction must be protected from premature criticism (Lakatos, 1970, p. 157):

> ... all this suggests that we must not discard a budding research programme, simply because it has so far failed to overtake a powerful rival. We should not abandon it if, supposing its rival were not there, it would constitute a progressive problem shift. And we should certainly regard a newly interpreted fact as a new fact, ignoring the insolent priority claims of amateur fact collectors. As long as a budding research programme can be rationally reconstructed as a progressive problems shift, it should be sheltered for a while from a powerful established rival.

This 'rational reconstruction' is Lakatos's intervention in the history of the sciences, his philosophical history for the sciences. The normative methodology that is produced by the philosophy produces a double history for the research programme: an *internal* history which in its reconstruction provides a rational account of the growth of objective knowledge, supplemented by an empirical *external* history. The former is given priority, and the latter is described as 'irrelevant for the understanding of science' (Lakatos, 1971, p. 92) – and (p. 106):

> External history either provides non-rational explanations of the speed, locality, selectiveness, etc. of historic events *as interpreted* in terms of internal history; or, when history differs from its rational reconstruction, it provides an empirical explanation of why it differs.

The problem that arises here is that the requirement within Lakatos's project for coherent programmes forces him to construct the research programmes as rational totalities whose internal history is governed by the demands of a logic that is not necessarily present or uniform. Set against this, the external history in its divergences is simply failing to engage with a *post hoc ergo propter hoc* logical construction, not with a specific body of theory. The kind of distinction which Lakatosian rationalism thereby imposes tends to revert to the internal–external distinction in the history of the sciences whose rejection was one of the progressive steps of Kuhn and Feyerabend (Feigl, 1974, p. 2). These problems are underlined if we go on to consider the actual histories that this approach has produced (Zahar, 1973; Latsis, 1972). These internal and external histories are not treated in an even-handed fashion, the external history being subordinated to the internal history in the order of analysis, the difference between them being regarded as the distinction between rational and non-rational orders. However, the rationality of the internal history depends not upon a consideration of the manner in which any given science orders its concepts and sets up their principles of coherence and validity, but is derived directly from the description that the scientific practice gives of itself. The categories proper to the methodology of research programmes, such as 'core', 'protective belt', 'negative and positive heuristic', 'progress' and 'degeneration', are simple descriptive categories which in the final analysis possess similar faults to those of the Kuhnian 'paradigm'. While initially appearing to give some basis for the construction of histories of the sciences, they in fact lead to the kind of equivocation between epistemology and sociology which is the dynamic which proliferates the definitions of 'paradigm' (Tribe, 1973, pp. 468–70). Research programmes resolve this dilemma by eliding a historical account of a science with the succession of statements that a given practice itself produces. The result is that Lakatosian history of science is a simple chronicle of theoretical events recording the minutiae of change but unable to effectively investigate the reasons for the variations that are thereby registered.

The use of this approach in the literature of the history of economics tends to confirm this judgment. Blaug's (1976) innovatory paper demonstrates the superiority of Lakatos over Kuhn, but then goes on to provide a Lakatosian Keynes which is reminiscent of the Kuhnian version noted above, in that the pay-off from this transcription process is not at all clear. O'Brien (1976, pp. 146–8), however, in a confrontation of Adam Smith with the Lakatosian methodology, noted the disturbing lack of specificity and discrimination that results from this procedure, developing some queries originally raised by Blaug. On the other hand, some of the contributions to a symposium of papers concerned with research programmes as a means of evaluation of contemporary theory located distinct programmes within quite specialised areas of neo-classical economics (Latsis, 1976). Such divergence indicates that the methodology does not contain within itself the necessary means for demarcating the unities that it constructs, nor does it provide any epistemological principles that articulate a domain of work.

The initially appealing methodology is thus little more than a formal apparatus of description whose positive value for the history of the sciences is little more than that of Kuhn's proposals. There is a great deal more philosophical rigour to the work of Lakatos of course, and also the manner in which the methodology is deployed leads to a detailed consideration of actual theories in a manner that *The Structure of Scientific Revolutions* never made possible. But this very philosophical rigour is the signature of the fate of the enterprise, since it simply repeats the attempt on the part of the philosophy of science to provide the discursive proofs that can only be produced in the science themselves. The principal concern of Lakatos, as of Popper, is to introduce criteria that can demarcate science from non-science. However, this activity is a philosophical one which attempts to specify the conditions under which discourses can be evaluated positively, specifying in advance the conditions of a sound methodology or an adequate history.

This self-appointed task of the philosophy of science, systematising contemporary discoveries in the physical sciences and demonstrating the continuity of such advances with previous work, was the object of Bachelard's investigations in the 1920s and 1930s. Bachelard characterised this as the general mode of operation of a philosophy of science with respect to the sciences: to validate, systematise, and evaluate the sciences by the pronouncements of a 'superior' discursive order. Bachelard's work represents a double intervention against, on the one hand, philosophy's treatment of the sciences, and on the other the histories which such philosophies validated. For this reason a brief discussion of his work provides a valuable counter to prevailing conceptions of the relation of philosophical discourse to economic discourse, and also directs attention to the principles of discursive analysis that in fact inform this book.[11]

For Bachelard, the object of a science is not something that is pre-given; it is something that is constructed in a radical discontinuity with the everyday world by the disposition of specific concepts. The theoretical nature of a science is not therefore a result of the powers of reasoning of an individual scientist, but is the property of the structure of the science itself. The science constructs its own principles and rules of evidence; they are not derivative of a 'philosophy'. This position permits authorial accounts of the history of the sciences to be rejected decisively, for the elements of which it is constituted are theoretical, that is, constructs which form part of a discursive structure (Bachelard, 1970, p. 19):

The first experience or, to speak more exactly, the first observation, is always a first obstacle for scientific culture. This first observation presents itself with a luxuriance of images; it is picturesque, concrete, natural, easy. It has only to be described to be wondered at. One thinks then one understands. We begin our investigation by characterising this obstacle and showing that there is rupture and not continuity between observation and experimentation.

Bachelard characterises the development of discursive formations as a process which contains within it the presence of what he terms 'epistemological obstacles' which intervene to block the process of theoretical development. His *Formation de l'esprit scientifique*, first published in 1938, is an exposition of a series of such obstacles present in eighteenth-century thought which systematically blocked the development of specific sciences by a set of images which prevented theorisation shifting from the given. These obstacles, as he pointed out, were not to be conceived as external conditions or the result of the feeble-mindedness of eighteenth-century thinkers: they are internal to the structure of the thought itself. He went on to outline a number of such obstacles: 'initial experience', 'general knowledge', imagery derived from the sponge and porosity, animism, and so on. Pre-scientific thought, argued Bachelard, is a ceaseless quest for unprincipled variety, formulating generalisations directly from the most hasty empirical observations, striving to make everything comparable with everything else. 'Laws' are formulated such as 'all bodies fall' and 'all living beings are mortal' – the writings of the eighteenth century are full of such attempts to begin an investigation by stating a set of definitions, which then actually prevent the possibility of a scientific investigation (Bachelard, 1970, p. 56).

The Bachelardian distinction between the sanctioned and the peripheral histories of a science have already been noted above; and in his own writings Bachelard concentrated mainly on an investigation of the sanctioned histories, apart from his *Psychoanalysis of Fire*, which is in effect an appendix to the *Formation*. The peripheral history remained, in general, unexamined, treated as a 'chamber of horrors', in Lecourt's term (1972, p. 35). We have to look outside Bachelard's work in order to discover more complete 'Bachelardian histories', and it will be useful to provide an outline of just one. For the positive aspects of Bachelardian history of science are by their nature irreducible to a set of formal principles – this is in fact their specific strength. The displacement of a positive methodology results in an inability to prescribe in the normal manner a 'historiography for the sciences'. Instead the analyses of the sciences must deal with the process of concept formation, forms of proof and forms of explanation within the structure of that science, and not according to logomachic prescriptions dreamed up by some ambitious philosopher seeking universal principles in the structure of the sciences.

The example that will be used here is Canguilhem's *La Formation du concept de réflexe aux XVIIᵉ et XVIIIᵉ siècles*, a book which openly proclaims itself as a recurrent history (1955, p. 167).[12] It addresses itself to the problem that in the late nineteenth century the concept of 'reflex' was conceived mechanistically; it was therefore concluded that the concept must have been 'discovered' by a mechanistic biologist. The history of physiology therefore nominated Descartes, who had proposed a mechanical theory of involuntary movement; from this it was concluded that Descartes had described, named and conceived a theory of reflex action. Some historians actually claim that Descartes used the word 'reflex', while others contend that the concept, but not the word, originated with Descartes (Canguilhem, 1955, pp. 37–8). Canguilhem underlines that when historians search in this way for the birth of a concept, they seek *words*, it being assumed that a concept is not only a word but also a substantive. It is possible to show that such assumptions mislead the historians, for the term 'reflex' was used as an adjective before it became a substantive, and it was even used in this way in the nineteenth century. The essential feature of a concept of reflex action is not simply to contain the outline of a mechanical explanation of muscular movement, it is to admit that part of the periphery of the organism is disturbed, which after reflection in a centre returns to the same periphery. The distinguishing characteristic of reflex action is that it does not originate in a centre, and it is in this that the distinction of voluntary from non-voluntary action lies. For Cartesian mechanics, however, a movement which appears at the periphery originates with the centre of centres, the cardiac passage. Canguilhem (1955, p. 52) proceeds to trace meticulously the source of the claims that place Descartes as the originator of the concept of reflex action, and examines the conditions for this source being constituted as the precursor of nineteenth-century physiology:

> If one finds in the work of Descartes the theoretical equivalent of certain tentative attempts to constitute, in the nineteenth century, a general reflexology, one does not find there, considered rigorously, either the term or the concept of reflex. It cannot be too heavily stressed that it is the explanation of the movements of the heart which contains the germ of the ruin of all Cartesian physiology.

Notice that Canguilhem states here that it is the *structure* of Cartesian physiology that prevents the formation of the concept of reflex action, and there then follows a careful examination of the evidence for this claim. He shows how the concept of reflex can be said to have originated with Willis, who like Descartes cast around for means of rendering intelligible the productions of organic phenomena, but within the framework of an energetics. The term is then shown in its passage through the eighteenth century inscribed within a vitalist framework, a framework which at this time organised the specific character of organic phenomena and played a progressive role in combating the Cartesian mechanistic conception of the organism. The vitalists of the eighteenth century were in fact positivists deploying vitalism to reject metaphysical theories of the essence of life; in doing this they rejected the mechanical notion of the organism, which by virtue of its concentration on the whole ('the machine') was not able to formulate the sub-elements except by straight borrowings from mechanical terminology (Canguilhem, 1955, pp. 113–27).

From this curt summary of some points that are raised in this exemplary discursive history, it can be seen that attention is repeatedly drawn to the structure within which concepts and explanation are formed, without at any point it being necessary to construct a unity or assess the forms of explanation according to some externally derived philosophical source. And it is this general approach to discourse analysis that will inform the arguments presented in this book, and which governs the non-historical nature of what might at a first glance appear to be a sophisticate's history of Classical Political Economy. This introductory chapter has been aimed at an elementary clearing of the ground, a softening-up exercise which has attempted to prevent certain conclusions forming before the argument gets under way.

It has been suggested at various points that economic discourse is the child of the nineteenth century, but a child without a history in the accepted sense of the term. How can such a history be constructed, a silent story of what is to be but not yet is? Instead of historical genesis, there will be found in the following pages a set of explanations of the foreclosure of the terrain of economics in the seventeenth and eighteenth centuries, demonstrating the necessity for this terrain to exist for a 'history' to come into being. For Ricardo, 'the past' can have no force; only when a discourse is constituted does its past rise up as an eternal presence. The economic discourse that forms in the early nineteenth century sets up conceptions of land and labour in a particular fashion to provide the bases of an economic analysis. However, these categories cannot be treated as eternities, the points at which a historical account can grasp to 'make sense' of the historicity of economic discourse. The categories 'land' and 'labour' are themselves constructed in the discourse; they do not precede it. And the following chapter, by considering the conjunction of these terms in the category 'rent', will show that these apparently eternal 'economic categories' are not invariant, that specific discursive conditions are required for these terms to flow freely together in the manner so often taken for granted in the writing of a history.

2

'Rent' as an Economic Category

For the most part this book concerns itself with the forms in which land and labour are constituted in various theoretical discourses. However, some remarks can be made at this point concerning the manner in which one particular economic category, 'rent', appears to place land and labour in a specific relation. By discussing the variability of this category it will be shown that there is no such unique configuration, and the term 'rent', which today is associated with land as a contractual object, has also been used for labour as the appropriate object. In addition to this, it will be shown in Chapter 6 that it is the theory of rent that is the theoretical core of Classical Political Economy; but the category that appears here is one constructed theoretically, and is not given to the theory historically. 'Rent' instead has no history, as is argued below. While it is central to Classical Political Economy, the term cannot be treated as an essence whose process of emergence is indicative of the genesis of Classical Economics. This chapter, then, seeks to begin the investigation which will establish such a claim.

The modern use of the term 'rent' denotes a payment related to contracts of hire in which the object hired is a building, land, or some kind of good. Such objects remain the property of the lessor throughout the term of the hire; the payments made by the lessee (the 'rent' of the object) do not entitle the lessee to acquisition of rights of property in the object without additional contractual stipulations. Consequently it is more accurate to say that it is not an object that is hired but rather the use of an object which is the property of another, the permissible modes of use being specified in the contract. With the termination of the contract the use-rights of the lessee lapse naturally, and on restoration to the owner the object can be hired out again to another party. It might appear at this point that the expenditure on an object which after a period reverts intact to another renders rental payment a particular form of revenue: he who actually uses the object, productively or unproductively, has to pay a sum of money for such use to an owner who can command such payment solely on the basis of legal title to the object. One party is able, by virtue of title to property, to gain a revenue produced by the productive employment of others, a situation which, as we will see later, was bitterly denounced by nineteenth-century radicals. However, it must not be forgotten that this separation of ownership from use is of benefit to capitalist enterprises that are thereby enabled to utilise resources without the necessity of purchasing them outright. In this way, land and buildings can be incorporated in a process of production without it being necessary to bear the cost and risks of ownership.

This configuration of use and ownership was characteristic of English agriculture from the early eighteenth century. The term 'rent', when used in the treatises and estate accounts of the period, refers to capitalist ground-rent, the payment of a sum of money for use-rights over farmland for a specified period, calculated at a rate of so many shillings per acre, and with the contractual responsibilities of each party stipulated in advance. If we go back to the preceding century, however, this precise matrix becomes dislocated: we find an object called 'quit-rent', associated with payments called 'fines', united not by the relation of landlord, tenant and land, but rather by the relation of landlord and tenant with land as an appendage. Unlike capitalist ground-rent, quit-rent is not expressed as so many shillings per acre, but rather is the let of a named farm or collection of lands. If we then go back to estate accounts of the medieval period, we find that land can be displaced altogether: a rent apparently paid for a piece of land can be transformed almost overnight into services performed by the holder unrelated to the land, or be calculated as so much produce without considering directly the capacity of the land supposedly the object of the transaction to bear the produce demanded. It appears therefore that agricultural rent is not a unitary economic category, despite the fact that a diverse array of payments are all termed 'rent' in manorial and estate accounts.

It would not be enough of course to simply register such variation; and in this chapter it will be briefly shown how 'rent' is variously constituted by distinct configurations of land and labour. Following from this, it will be shown that a theory of distribution constructed around a theory of rent, in the manner of Ricardian theory, cannot be constituted for a feudal economy. It is almost commonplace to argue that a theory of distribution specific to a capitalist economy cannot be transferred to a feudal economy; however, such an assertion leaves open the possibility that a theory of feudal distribution could in principle be formulated. It will be argued below that no such analogue to a theory of capitalist distribution can be constructed for feudalism, for the categories of feudal economy repeatedly disperse the terms and relations implicated in such a theory. Such dispersion can be demonstrated with the category of 'rent', a term which has no essential referent or unity apart from specific discursive relations. There can therefore be no such thing as a 'history' of rent, for this word fluctuates and dissolves before attempts to construe an essential meaning for it. A history of rent theory would further presuppose that an economic discourse exists as an eternity within which this category occupies a reserved space. But a theory of rent, a major component of a theory of distribution, cannot exist outside of the discourse which sets it to work; and a history of rent theory thus has as much meaning as a history of medieval aircraft production, or an account of Elizabethan speedway racing.

The conception of agricultural rent which has prevailed from the eighteenth century corresponds to the set of relations outlined at the beginning of this chapter. A lessee (the tenant) hires land from a lessor (the landlord), and uses the land so hired to engage in the production of agricultural commodities. The lessee pays to the lessor a sum of money which is termed 'rent', calculated as a sum per acre plus other payments for materials supplied by the landlord, buildings and other elements. Such subsidiary payments and non-financial covenants that the landlord imposes on the tenant (such as courses, improvements etc.) are summarised in the conception of the rental relation as a contractual one between free economic agents. The level of the rent paid is related to the productivity of the land − or, more exactly, is a function of the mechanism determining the prices of the commodities produced on that land.[1] The existence of rent is in this case intricately related to land, the tenant further being a capitalist whose task is to organise the deployment of labour on this land for the effective functioning of the production process. This is of course very schematically stated, and we will see in later chapters how this configuration of land and labour is often expressed in conceptions of the land itself as the producer of commodities; rent is, as a consequence, not treated as the payment made on the basis of organised social production using land, but rather as a natural product, a 'gift of Nature'. In such conceptions, the terms 'land' and 'labour' carry a connotation of a confrontation of the natural world with the social − or even of the powers of Nature/God with the powers of Man.

The existence of rent presupposes that possession of land is divorced from the activity of using it productively, such that rent can be seen as a wedge separating man from the land. The almost mystical bond that is associated with notions of land and its ownership is one which has been the subject of popular agitation for centuries, for the possession of land is associated with the freedom of the individual, who retains by virtue of such possession the means of subsistence. Separation from the land symbolises the necessity to work for others in order to gain a subsistence, and is usually conceived as an unnatural state of affairs. It cannot be said that this separation is characteristic solely of capitalist production, for it is clear that popular agitation around the possession of land has existed spasmodically since the sixteenth century in England. But the payment of rent for land on a systematic basis symbolises the existence of capitalist relations of production in agriculture which separate the producers from effective possession of the principal means of production (and also, of course, subsistence).

If we turn to feudal relations, however, this precise formation in which land worked by labour bears a specific rent no longer applies – and the term 'feudal rent' denotes a dislocation from the land and a gravitation of the referent of 'rent' to labour. If we examine manorial accounts of the thirteenth or fourteenth centuries, the existence of 'rent' and its association with a named subject and a piece of land is quite clear; but this rent can undergo some peculiar transformations, and the amount of rent paid has little or nothing to do with the price of saleable agricultural produce, or even with the extent of land occupied. This 'feudal rent' is in fact not a rent of land, but is an expression of the subordination of feudal labour. As a consequence of this, it is really quite accidental that feudal and capitalist rents can appear to be variants of a particular category. In order to understand the nature of this feudal rent, it is necessary to devote some space to an outline of what can be roughly termed a 'feudal economy'.[2]

Feudalism is associated with a system of dependent land-holding in which the grant of land to a tenant is in return for services, in particular military services. This is, as it were, a microcosm of a set of relations repeated up and down a political hierarchy, for the grant of land begins with the king and then by a process of sub-infeudation the tenures are subdivided. A consequence of this arrangement is that only the king owns land in a manner approximating to modern conceptions of ownership; everyone else 'holds of' his superior and is bound by this relation to specified services.[3] But to term this form of property 'ownership', even in the case of the king, obscures the manner in which tenure is defined, the conditions under which it is allocated and surrendered. If we say that the king owns all the land, it would be assumed nowadays that this entitles the king to dispose of the land as he wished with respect to its leasing, sale, and so on. But these contractual arrangements are not necessary components of a form of property in land: hiring and selling of an economic object are not requisite rights vested in the title-holder to give that holder adequate property in the object. To state that a legal subject has title to an object is not to say that that subject is also endowed with the rights of hire and sale over that object to another party. Of course it might be the case that limited rights of sale or hire are specified, for example within kin-groups, and so on; but the absence of such universal rights in no way implies that the property in the object is in some fashion incomplete or divided. The important consequence from the point of view of the present discussion is that title to land vested in a specified individual (so-called 'private ownership') does not necessarily mean that such land can be hired out or sold. And this is exactly the case with feudal property in land, for under prevailing conceptions of property and the allocation of rights in land, the form of contractual relation specified at the beginning of this chapter cannot be formulated. Capitalist ground-rent cannot exist in a feudal economy because (put simply) there is no title-holder who is in a position to hire out land. The form of property in land does not comprehend the leasing arrangements that under different conditions were thought as natural concomitants to property in land. And in certain circumstances, the association of the term 'property' with other legal and social statuses of the subject would result in a proposal to purchase a piece of land from a person appearing equivalent to a proposal to buy the person himself. The diversification of the term 'property' as pertaining principally to economic objects occurs in the eighteenth century; and if this conception is read back into previous social and economic orders the nature of these formations is necessarily misconstrued.

This complex of rights, possession and forms of property is central to the feudal economy, and rests ultimately on two basic supports: the status of persons; and the disposition of rights over land. If we look, for example, at the sources of evidence for the feudal economy – the Domesday Book, the Hundred Rolls of 1279, the 1517 Inquisition – we find here that the principal concern is to establish the form of the economy by a process of assigning rights over objects and persons to their proper holders. As Kosminsky (1956, p. 13) argues with respect to the Hundred Rolls, the purpose of this great survey was to re-establish the respective rights of the king, the lords and the freemen after a period of great social and economic upheaval during which the rights of the Crown had been eroded. Accordingly the investigation sought to determine the forms of authorisation possessed by those who had acquired Crown land, and the summary provided by Kosminsky (1956, p. 12) provides a unique image of the forms and order of property.

> The commissioners were charged to make investigation into the following matters: what holdings were held by each archbishop, bishop, abbot, prior, earl, baron, knight, freeman or townsman in the cities, boroughs, townships and villages; what castles they had, what knight's fees, land-holdings, demesnes, woods, meadows, parks, pastures (common and private), preserves for hunting, fairs, markets; what were their revenues from rents, from villein holdings, from cottars, from labour services done by serfs; from waters, common and private fisheries, rivers, fish-ponds, mills, gardens, heaths, marshes, peat-beds, alder-groves etc. Inquiry is to be made as to who holds his estate in fee and who by fee-farm, who for life and who for a term of years, who holds of the king in chief and who of other lords, and in the latter case which lords and for what services or payments. Further, the inquiry is to discover what demesnes, freeholders, villeins, serfs, cottars and other tenants each of the aforementioned parties possesses, and whether they hold immediately of their lords or through mesne tenants; it is to establish also the size of the holding of each free man, villein, serf or cottar, and its terms, that is from whom held and against what services or dues; and to find out which fees and other holdings should pay scutage and how much, who holds these fees, on what conditions and from what date.

The purpose of this cadastral survey was to establish who held what and by what title, in particular seeking to arrive at an estimate of the resources of the king. From this juxtaposition of persons and things conceived according to their forms of assignation (persons to feudal superiors, things to their holders), we get a delineation of the contemporary social formation under the rubric of a census of property in which the status of persons and things is not distinguished.[4] The feudal world is a world of property and rights of possession, and subordinates in this delineation of agents of possession the world of persons. In this configuration land plays a central role as the most crucial form of property, necessary for the reproduction of the persons existing in this world, but, even more vital, necessary to solidify the complexes of allegiances that made up the feudal political order. Gregory King, in his seventeenth-century survey, conceived the nation as a set of property-holding classes, but within the broad classes that he used his principal concern was the enumeration of persons. In contrast to this, the number of persons in the kingdom is almost incidental to the commissioners of 1279; they are concerned to establish the forms of property and extent of possessions.

Vinogradoff, in his classic study *Villeinage in England*, emphasises that the legal status of villeins was not related to the connection of the villein to the land but to his relation with a lord, and only as a consequence of this to a piece of land. This treatment of the villein as the property in some way of the lord in fact led Bracton (Vinogradoff, 1892, p. 47) to equate in law the English villein and the Roman slave, and consequently to use the terms *servus*, *villanus* and *nativus* indiscriminately. While this ignores the limitation of the powers of the lord over the villein, more importantly such an elision obscures the differential modes of proof required to establish possession of particular categories of villeins. Certain kinds of villein, termed *in gross*, were held absolutely and without reference to any other; some, termed *regardant*, for whom no confession or deed of bondage existed, could only be impleaded with respect to a particular manor (Vinogradoff, 1892, pp. 57–8):

> The possession of a manor carries the possession of cultivators with it. It is always important to decide whether a bondsman is in the seisin of his lord or not, and the chief means to show it is to trace his connection with the territorial lordship. The interposition of the manor in the relation between master and man is, of course, a striking feature and it gives a very characteristic turn to medieval servitude. But if it is not consistent with the general theory laid down in the thirteenth century law books, it does not lead to anything like the Roman *colonatus*. The serf is not placed on a particular plot of land to do definite services under the protection of the State. He may be shifted from one plot within the jurisdiction of his lord to another, from one area of jurisdiction to another, from rural labour to industrial work or house work, from one set of customs and services to another.

Thus this personal dependence is not unconditional; it can only be effected via a territorial basis, such that the possession and occupation of land is determined according to relations of superiority and subordination with which it is associated, but of which it is not constitutive.

This is expressed in the organisation of the manor, which while having a territorial basis is not a geographical entity but a legal one. The manor is the unit of authority of a particular lord, and the land which pertains to this might be split into diverse forms and be quite scattered. For example, it used to be thought that 'a manor' was made up of the lord's land (demesne), villein land, and freeholder's land. The villein divided his labour between work on his own land and work on the lord's, with various services like carting included. However, Kosminsky (1956, pp. 84–5) showed from the Hundred Rolls (derived not from a manorial unit of analysis but rather from a vill-based investigation) that this so-called 'typical' manor was only one variant – there existed manors with no villein, or no demesne land, or some with only demesne land. In addition to this the manor had no necessary geographical integrity, any one vill being divided between two, three or even more manors. This institution is thus an expression of feudal property, in which the disposition of land is a secondary consideration to the ranking and subordination of a political order.

This is underlined by a closer consideration of the nature of feudal rent which expresses this characteristic in the forms of the variation it undergoes. Kosminsky (1956, p. 136) distinguishes three forms of feudal income that can be found recorded in manorial and government records: *redditus assisae*, an annual fixed money rent, forming the larger part of the rent of free tenants and usually a certain part of the rent of villeins; *opera* or *consuetudines*, obligations to labour on the part of villeins and, to a certain extent, free tenants; and annual contributions in kind made by both classes, sometimes given in the records with an indication of a monetary equivalent. Certain other payments from dependents to lords were paid on occasions like the death of a tenant or the entry of a new lord or king. All these forms of revenue are generally referred to as 'feudal rent', and as can be seen the basis on which these payments are made is one of a general subordination in which land plays a quite incidental role. Various permutations are of course possible among the three principal forms, and accounts can be found of the payments being made entirely in money, labour or produce. The choice on the part of the lord as to the form the composition of his revenue took depended on prevailing conditions – if, for example, a manor lay in the vicinity of a town (measured in terms of days' cartage), it could be worth while to directly convert produce into money for purchase of luxury goods by extracting rent in the form of labour services and then selling the produce in town; or, on the other hand, the lord could dispense with demesne cultivation altogether and simply exact produce rents, again disposing of the revenue by sale in a town. Naturally this form of calculation depended on the differing degrees of productivity of labour services as against produce rents, and the degree of control that was available to the feudal administration.

It has sometimes been suggested that the appearance of payment of rent in money indicates a transformation of feudal rent into capitalist rent, in which the growth of monetary relations encourages the development of local markets and the emergence of production for sale in these markets. Kosminsky makes clear that such an implication cannot be simply read into the existence of money rents, and as Hilton (1947, pp. 22, 85) has shown with some Leicestershire ecclesiastical estates tithe income (analogous to produce rent) was leased to entrepreneurs for cash since it was impractical to transport grain over any distance. The disposal of grain piecemeal in local markets did not therefore have any repercussions on a regional market, and in addition the revenue from such sale was transferred to a great extent via the leasing arrangement to the towns. Duby (1968, p. 237) discusses the exigencies which could lead to the conversion of rents into the money form and points to the increasing indebtedness of the lord's economy as the major imperative:

> For many lords the most pressing problem was to obtain money, and this led them to demand cash rather than labour or agricultural produce from their tenants and men. The conversion of services and dues offered a simple and immediate solution to the problem of finance. It was acceptable, if not to all, then at least to the most enterprising peasants, who were prepared to pay money provided they could dispose of their crops and profit from the growing opportunities for taking their surplus to market.

However, this 'surplus' that Duby refers to is no fixed amount, for it does not follow that the value of the crops directly rendered, the price of crops sold in order to render money rent, and the value of the services performed by the feudal peasant, are in any way comparable. Indeed, the shifting from one to the other on the part of the lord presupposes that advantages are to be gained from one form over another: there is no unitary surplus which simply takes on different forms. Kula (1976, pp. 29 ff.) has shown that the 'value' of feudal labour services is quite distinct from the 'price' of these services commuted into money rents, and that there is no way in which a price can be assigned to the services performed. The existence of monetary forms of exchange in certain regions of an economy does not imply that even the monetary values assigned to particular goods are uniform or comparable, while the exchanges that are only spasmodically monetised can not by virtue of this be assigned a meaningful price.

From the point of view of capitalist production, feudal rent is a dispersed and heterogeneous category, referring only tangentially to land, and even in this reference the revenue flow is not associated with a contractual relation which takes land as the object. Capitalist ground-rent is therefore a quite distinct form from feudal rent, and should in no way be conceived as a more 'specific' variant of a universal rental form which is the mark of all agrarian economies. Feudal rent is in fact the manner in which persons are constituted into feudal relations of property, the form of accommodation which takes place between a real world of property relations and the persons who have to enter this world. The magnitude of this feudal rent (however calculated) is not subject to any unique form of economic determination, but is rather the outcome of prevailing political domination and certain calculations flowing from this. As a result of this situation it is not possible to construct a theory of distribution for the feudal economy which comprehends effectively this rental relationship. 'Economic categories' in the feudal world thus have a determination which escapes the realm of the economy, and thus cannot be united and systematised into a particular form of argument or constitute an economic discourse.

It is not being argued here that the nature of the feudal economy conditions the non-possibility of economic discourse existing in the medieval world. Rather, it has been argued that the form of representation of economic processes in court and manorial records, organised as they are according to particular legal categories, interdicts the formation of a realm of the economic which is the object of state administration. When monarchs wished to assess the 'state of the nation' they turned to an exhaustive process of stock-taking and demarcation of property rights in which neither an economy is directly given, nor the persons who occupy the legal categories which are the object of investigation. Later in the seventeenth and eighteenth centuries such investigations turned on the enumeration of persons, as we will see in Chapter 5. But in the feudal world, such persons are invisible beneath an elaboration of forms of property and the proper assignation of titles to property, in which the object of property is indifferently 'thing' or 'person'.

This chapter has argued that the term 'rent' is not an economic category with a unilateral application in agrarian economies, for the conditions of existence of rent as a relation linking land and labour and at the same time dividing them are not eternally given. By focusing on this term it has been possible to indicate the existence of a series of disjunctions between the discursive and the non-discursive, and between discursive forms themselves, that will begin to be elaborated in the following chapters. By next examining seventeenth-century notions of property we will see some of the problems involved in the constitution of land as economic property, and labour as the form in which title to property is assigned.

3

Property, Patriarchy and the Constitution of a Polity

The preceding chapter has contended that the existence of the term 'rent' does not require that this term is constituted as an economic category. In this chapter attention is shifted from single categories to the terrain on which such terms are projected. The problem to be discussed here concerns the conditions of formation of an economic discourse, and seeks to show that these conditions are not to be found in the literature of the seventeenth century. Indeed, the category 'seventeenth-century economics' is constituted in the history of economics as a problematic period of emergence, marked by special pleading on the part of various seventeenth-century authors who fail ultimately to develop a systematic approach to the subject (Letwin, 1963). However, it is not questioned that these diverse tracts represent the birth pangs of an economic science. Subsequent to the imposition of modern conceptions of economic analysis, such writings can be registered as confused, or lacking logical form. These shortcomings can then in turn be related to the prevailing cultural context, a form of argument which makes it possible to preserve an origin for economics while admitting its tentative nature.

There is, however, no 'economy' in seventeenth-century discourse; that is, the terrain on which contemporary economic concepts and forms of explanation exist undiscovered, or more precisely is not constituted. Notions of exchange, production, property, distribution, price, value, all can be traced in dispersed writings of this period. But in every case these words are not the terms of neo-classicism, nor even of Classical Political Economy; they cannot therefore be united by such anachronistic unities. If such terms do at some point exist in a loose relation, it is within a quite distinct discursive space: that of political argument, centring on the justification of the monarchy and the nature of a commonwealth. Very generally we find here the nearest approximation to a conception of 'an economy' susceptible to discursive representation. But the 'economy' is merely constructed in the course of establishing a body politic, and as will be shown cannot be conceived independently of this.

However, it has been suggested that this political argument is conditional upon certain distinct economic conceptions associated with an emergent capitalist economy. In this way Macpherson (1962) has proposed that the political thought of Hobbes, Harrington, the Levellers and Locke presupposes a conception of 'possessive individualism', that the political subject of these writers is bourgeois man implicated in a series of market relations. According to Macpherson, then, the theories of Hobbes and Locke are expressive of certain problems of a capitalist economy, and can in a limited way be treated as representative of this economy. It will be shown in this chapter that the primary error of such an approach is to misconstrue the constitution of economic and political categories in Hobbes and Locke.[1] The theories of property proposed by Hobbes and Locke are concerned with the constitution of political agents. Macpherson argues that a particular (bourgeois) conception of an economic agent is required to effect this, a 'possessive individual' whose condition of existence is a market society which, according to Macpherson, is characteristic of seventeenth-century England. By demonstrating the patriarchal framework within which economic categories are formulated in the seventeenth century it will be shown in this chapter that conceptions of a market society could not play such a major role in political argument, and that the apparent 'economic conceptions' identified by Macpherson are subject to a dispersion that resists any attempt to identify 'seventeenth-century economic discourse'.

The general category of 'patriarchalism' serves to delineate a means in the seventeenth century of forming arguments concerning the just organisation of that which is political. While a heritage for such conceptions of social organisation can be traced to Plato and Aristotle, patriarchy became in the seventeenth century a central and indispensable element in the defence of monarchy and the rejection of republican ideas (Pocock, 1957). But it did not only serve those who constructed arguments in the defence of the Crown; the contractualist opponents also depended on a patriarchal conception of the political order, as Macpherson (1962, ch. III) has shown with respect to the Levellers, for instance. As we shall see, this patriarchal form of thought informed conceptions of economy, being the primary means for the constitution of the basic economic units of production and circulation.

Plato had argued that the large household and the small-size city were analogous with respect to the exercise of authority, basing the exercise of public power by the sovereign on an analogy with the (natural) authority of the father of the family. In the latter case the authority deriving from paternity was extended to wives, servants and slaves, such that the authority was exercised over a household made up of persons of differing legal statuses and powers. Aristotle's disagreement with this was concerned with the simple equation that Plato made, and he argued that it was a mistake to associate the statesman with the monarch and the manager of a household in a unilateral fashion. But as in Locke's critique of Filmer, which as we shall see in many ways replicated these positions, the denial of a simple patriarchal order in society is accompanied by a more subtle re-establishment (Schochet, 1975, pp. 19–22).

Bodin's *Six Books of the Commonwealth*, originally published in 1576, is a good example of the centrality of these conceptions for the establishment of political discourse, for he begins his explication of the nature of a commonwealth with a discussion of the family, in which the basic principles at issue are clearly stated (n.d., pp. 6–7):

> A family may be defined as the right ordering of a group of persons
> owing obedience to a head of household, and of those interests which
> are his proper concern. The second term of our definition of the
> commonwealth refers to the family because it is not only the true
> source and origin of the commonwealth, but also its principal
> constituent. Xenophon and Aristotle divorced economy or household
> management from police or disciplinary power, without good reason
> to my mind ... I understand by domestic government the right
> ordering of family matters, together with the authority which the
> head of the family has over his dependents, and the obedience due
> from them to him, things which Aristotle and Xenophon neglect.
> Thus the well-ordered family is a true image of the commonwealth,
> and domestic comparable with sovereign authority. It follows that the
> household is the model of right order in the commonwealth.

The family is the basis of social order both by analogy and in terms of forming the basic elements of this order. The authority which the sovereign commands is an extension of the fourfold relationship within the family, between husband and wife, father and child, master and servant, and owner and slave (Bodin, n.d., p. 10):

> From the moment a marriage is consummated the woman is subject
> to her husband, unless he is still living as a dependent in his father's
> house. Neither slaves nor other dependents have any authority over

their wives, still less over their children. They are all subject to the
head of the family until such time as he shall have given his married
son his independence. No household can have more than one head,
one master, one seigneur. If there were more than one head there
would be a conflict of command and incessant family disturbances ...
wherefore a woman marrying a man still living in his father's house is
subject to her father-in-law.

The natural right of the father to command all members of the
household in this way derives from his being formed in the image of
God, who is the father of all things. In the private realm of the family the
power of the father is then absolute, just as in the public realm the power
of the sovereign body (in Bodin's case) is. But this public realm is itself
constituted by these heads of households, for by virtue of being free men
the heads of households can associate as equals. As Bodin (n.d., p. 18)
states, 'In so doing he ceases to be a master and becomes a citizen, and a
citizen may be defined as a free subject dependent on the authority of
another.'

It is clear from the foregoing that the same kind of argument can be
used to argue for both monarchy and commonwealth, for the authority
of the ruling body is in both cases derivative of the authority of heads of
households, who furthermore are constituted as political agents by
virtue of this status. The term 'patriarchy' does not then refer simply to a
conception of 'fatherly' or 'husbandly' power (and even less of course to
male power); the family group over which the patriarch rules is
extended to a household which includes servants and slaves.
'Household' and 'family' are not therefore the same thing – it is the first
which is of crucial concern.[2] This is clear from the use that Sir Thomas
Smith makes of the term in his *De Republica Anglorum* of 1583, where
he states that 'the house' includes the man, the woman, their children,
their servants, both bond and free, their cattle, 'their households stuffe,
and all other things, which are reckoned in their possession, so long as
all these remain together in one' (Smith, 1906, p. 23). The household is
consequently an autonomous political and economic unit, not requiring
the establishment of any external relations of power or subsistence in
order to meet its discursive conditions of existence. The importance of
this form of definition will become clear when we deal with authorship
in Hobbes and possession in Locke.

It was Filmer (1949, p. 57) who in the 1630's revived the Platonic
version of the patriarchal order, and buttressed it with arguments drawn
from the Old Testament:

I see then not how the children of Adam, or of any man else, can be free from subjection to their parents. And this subordination of children is the fountain of all regal authority, by the ordination of God himself. From whence it follows, that civil power, not only in general is by Divine institution, but even the assigning of it specifically to the eldest parent.

In *Patriarcha* Filmer argued that the power of the monarch derived from literal paternity of his people, so that the authority of the parent and the authority of the statesman were one and the same. All forms of social obedience were construed in terms of the patriarchal family (Laslett, 1949, p. 26), and indeed so were all forms of social organisation. This position became in the early 1680s one of the main theoretical buttresses of the monarchy and the Tory party, and it was against the political use of these arguments that Locke composed his *First Treatise of Government* in 1679–80, a work which was a detailed rebuttal of the Filmerian interpretation of patriarchy.

Locke addressed himself primarily here to the question of Adam as the first patriarch, the property vested in him by God, and the relation of paternal to political power. While showing the incoherence and contradictions of Filmer's arguments, it cannot be said that Locke breaks absolutely with the ground that Filmer establishes. This can be seen by comparing two sections from different parts of the *Two Treatises*. For example, in Chapter VI of the *First Treatise*, which is entitled 'The False Principles and Foundation of Sir Robert Filmer, and his Followers, are Detected and Overthrown', Locke employs his workmanship model to show that if parents make their children and thereby have just dominion over them, the father has equal dominion with the mother. In fact Locke goes as far as to claim that on this basis the mother has the greater share of dominion, since she has more to do with the making of the child. He continues this genetic form of argument in the following chapter, where it is suggested that if begetting is the source of authority, then a person cannot be subject to one who has not begotten him. But if we turn to chapter VI in the *Second Treatise*, entitled 'Of Paternal Power', we find that the mother is hardly touched on, and takes no part in the proof of the argument. And in the following chapter, it is stated that any differences between the husband and the wife are resolved by the husband, since rule 'naturally falls to the Man's share, as the abler and the stronger' (Locke, 1960, p. 364). Now it is quite clear that Locke is able to produce a sharp and effective criticism of Filmer's derivation of political power from paternal power, and show that it depends on a set of specious arguments. However, Locke does retain the patriarchal conception of the household, and this is clear from passages in the *Second Treatise* dealing with political and civil society and the possession of property (Locke, 1960, pp. 365–9, 328–30). As far as the latter is concerned, Tully (1977, p. 181) has pointed out that 'to appropriate' for Locke means to bring into the family, even though this right to possession derives from the maker's right. The issues involved here will of course be returned to below; and in dealing in more detail with the work of Hobbes and Locke it will be clear how crucial the conception of patriarchal order is for their constitution of political and economic agents.

As has been suggested above, Macpherson in his influential book argues the contrary position, stating that these agents are 'bourgeois individuals'.[3] In particular, he seeks to show, as we shall see, that the 'natural man' of Hobbes is bourgeois man, a node in a system of exchanges within 'possessive market society' (Macpherson, 1962, p. 48):

> By possessive market society I mean one in which, in contrast to a society based on custom and status, there is no authoritative allocation of work and rewards, and in which, in contrast to a society of independent producers who exchange only their products in the market, there is a market in labour as well as in products. If a single criterion of the possessive market society is wanted it is that a man's energy and skill are his own, yet are regarded not as integral parts of his personality, but as possessions, the use and disposition of which he is free to hand over to others for a price. It is to emphasise this characteristic of the fully market society that I have called it the *possessive* market society.

For Macpherson, the market is a mechanism which mediates the relation between commodity owners, and regulates the terms on which exchanges are made. The agents in possession of commodities are individuals seeking to maximise their utilities, some agents having a higher level of utilities than others, and some agents having more energy, skill and possessions than others. The capacity to labour is vendible, as is land (Macpherson, 1962, pp. 53–5). The freedom of the individual is the ability to enter voluntarily into contractual relations with other individuals with a view to the individual's interest. Political society is constituted to safeguard the individual's property in his own person and goods, and thus to safeguard the orderly relations of exchange between these individuals (Macpherson, 1962, pp. 262–3). It is clear that this is considered to be an adequate description of capitalist economic organisation, and that Macpherson wishes to argue that these capitalist relations are constitutive of the political theory of Hobbes and Locke. It is not proposed here to argue with Macpherson's description of capitalist or bourgeois society, although it can be pointed out that it is highly questionable. It is, however, already evident from this brief outline that 'man' in Hobbes and Locke is treated as designating an individual whose social bonds are simply those of the market society. Since 'man' is equivalent to 'individual' there is no need for Macpherson to consider the conditions of formation of this agent, since he already exists in the shape of the human person *qua* human being. The conditions of existence of this human person can then be treated as the reality of the economy within which the person exists. Macpherson asserts that this is a capitalist economy: thus 'man' becomes the vehicle on which we travel from the discursive order of *Leviathan* and the *Two Treatises* to the everyday world of the non-discursive.[4] This will now be demonstrated with respect to these two texts.

Macpherson's general argument with respect to Hobbes is that, while constructing a model of 'man', he presupposes capitalist relations as the conditions of existence of this agent. Hobbes 'man' is thus a bourgeois individual, and Hobbes 'civil society' is capitalist society (Macpherson, 1968, p. 50):

> The fact that he was, in his economic proposals, a seventeenth-century mercantilist, believing that positive state policy was needed to promote capitalist development, should not be allowed to obscure the fact that the economic model which he takes for granted (however much he disliked some aspects of it, as we shall see) is a fully capitalist model. He takes for granted that labour is a commodity, which proposition is the central criterion of capitalism: he states, incidentally to a discussion of foreign trade, that 'a man's labour also, is a commodity exchangeable for benefit, as well as any other thing'. And he derides the precapitalist concepts of commutative and distributive justice, on the grounds that they are meaningless as soon as one realises that the value of everything, including human beings, is determined by the market. Hobbes not only accepted market determination of value as a fact, he accepted it as right, in the sense that he could see no other moral basis for establishing the value of anything.

The problem with this construction that Hobbes makes on the relations of capitalist society is that he did not fully recognise the role of the division of this society into classes. This deficiency is argued, by Macpherson (1962, p. 93) to mar Hobbes's writings, the deficit with respect to the model of a market society resulting in a view of society as a fragmented entity. Consequently, the civil society that Hobbes constructs is fatally flawed at precisely the points where it fails to express adequately the conditions of the possessive market model. But if this hypothesis is seriously questioned, it can be shown that the manner in which Hobbes constitutes political agents does not depend on the model of capitalist society that Macpherson provides.

Hobbes's 'Leviathan', which he alternatively calls a commonwealth or a state, is described as 'but an Artificial Man; though of greater stature and strength than the Naturall, for whose protection and defence it was intended' (Hobbes, 1968, p. 81). The famous frontispiece to this text depicts a monarch bearing in one hand a sword and in the other a bishop's staff, looming over a town, villages and the countryside. The body of this monarch is made up of an assembly of men, emphasising the relation between the sovereign body and the body politic. Two questions arise here: one of the connection between the sovereign and the people; and one concerning the manner in which this 'people' is constituted. It is perhaps the second which is of most importance here.

The argument of *Leviathan* develops in three principal phases. First, we have 'Of Man', which delineates a basic nature of man and natural laws of mankind, the relation of this to language and the principles for the formation of true and false statements. In the second part is to be found an analysis of the political order of a commonwealth, the laws according to which it functions and the means available to it for the rectification of transgression. Finally, Parts Three and Four develop an argument based in theology and justification of the foregoing from scripture. Given that Hobbes sets out from a conception of 'man', it cannot be simply assumed that this 'man' is congruent with male persons. Macpherson does not of course assume this: he argues that this 'man' is a possessive individual, not a male person, formed by the capitalist relations within which he is implicated.

In the final chapter of Part One, Hobbes does consider the nature of this personality. There we find a person defined as 'he *whose words or actions are considered, either as his own, or as representing the words or actions of an other man, or of any other thing to whom they are attributed, whether Truly or by Fiction*' (Hobbes, 1968, p. 217). Note the way in which it is another *man* which is designated as an authoritative person for a subordinate, and this interjection can be taken to imply that when Hobbes talks of personality it is equivalent to talking of man. The distinction between truth and fiction that Hobbes makes concerns this notion of personality, for he argues that when words are considered to be those of the person, then this is a natural person, and when the words represent those of another, this involves an artificial person. There are grounds in the following passages for equating 'artificiality' with 'fictional'; in any case, the author of represented words or actions cannot, argues Hobbes, be an inanimate object such as a church, hospital, or bridge, for these things can only be personated by designated offices like Rector, Master, or Overseer.[5] It is the human agent in this office who gives authority to actors, not the office itself. The relation between author and actor is outlined as follows (Hobbes, 1968, p. 218):

> Of Persons Artificiall, some have their words and actions *Owned* by those whom they represent. And then the Person is the *Actor*; and he that owneth his words and actions, is the AUTHOR: in which case the Actor acteth by Authority ... And as the Right of possession, is called Dominion; so the Right of doing any Action, is called AUTHORITY. So that by Authority, is always understood a Right of doing any act: and *done by Authority*, done by Commission, or Licence from him whose right it is.

Apart from the institutions and objects mentioned above that Hobbes considers cannot be authors, there are some human beings excluded as well: namely, children, fools and madmen 'that have no use of Reason', and these categories may be personated by Guardians or Curators (Hobbes, 1968, p. 219). While women are not specifically excluded at this point, it is clear from the drift of the argument that their qualifications for personality are likely to be severely restricted, and we shall see that this is in fact the case.

The form of representation that is involved in the commonwealth is also considered under the same terms, and it is stressed that it is the function of representation which creates the unity of civil society. The unity of the multitude does not inhere in them by virtue of their common humanity, but is only to be found in the unity of the representer (Hobbes, 1968, p. 220). The condition of existence of civil society is therefore a sovereign person or body (in the latter case ruling by majority decision). The authority of this Representative as actor is provided by the covenants of natural law. But the nature of this 'multitude' who find their unity only in the sovereign is still unclear. Macpherson (1965, p. 181) does at times imply that these men are simple individuals, and he uses the terms interchangeably. But it is necessary to take the gender of this 'man' more seriously. Macpherson proposes that this 'man' is not the universal subject that Hobbes supposes, but a historical subject of a particular form of society – capitalism. While agreeing that 'man' is not universal but qualified, it is necessary to make another form of qualification concerning this political agent. While it is never explicitly stated in major passages in *Leviathan*, it can be suggested that far from civil society being constituted as a collectivity of possessing individuals whom Hobbes chooses to call 'men', it is in fact constituted as a collectivity of households whose heads are the political agents of political society by virtue of being heads of households (which is of course not the same thing as being the head of a family). These heads of households are authors by virtue of this status. The subordinate members of a household are not 'persons', that is, political agents. It is these households, and not possessing individuals, who represent the economic agents of political theory, and the manner in which these households are constituted cannot be simply reduced to a prevailing form of economic organisation. This will be shown in more detail in the following chapters.

While the household and the monarchy are not considered by Hobbes to be strictly analogous, it is the question of size and strength which is seen as the major principle of difference (1968, p. 257). If for example a large family exists independently of a commonwealth, it is

> of it self, as to the Rights of Soveraignty, a little Monarchy; whether that Family consist of a man and his children; or of a man and his servants; or of a man, his children, and servants together: wherein the Father or Master is Soveraign.

Elsewhere, cities and kingdoms are described as 'greater families' (ibid., p. 224) and in another text the early form of society is assumed to have been organised on strictly patriarchal lines (Hobbes, 1971, p. 159). Again, when speaking of the right of dominion over the child, Hobbes states that the power should belong equally to both parents by virtue of generation. But he goes on to argue that no man can serve two masters, and while it is incorrect to attribute to the man the dominion by virtue of his superior sex, Civil Law usually vests it in the father since 'for the most part Common-wealths have been erected by the Fathers' (Hobbes, 1968, p. 253). As has already been stressed above, there is not a unitary form of patriarchalism in the seventeenth century, since it was possible to take up quite diverse positions based on it, from extreme monarchism to radical democracy. Unlike many others, Hobbes eschews a construction of a civil society by argument from origins of society in general, but rather seeks these origins in the nature of man and the consequent necessity of civil society. It appears therefore that his political argument does not rest on patriarchal modes of reasoning but on a new discovery of man-as-object. However, the qualification for being a man in civil society is that one is a little monarch in a household. The sovereign then represents the 'people' by virtue of the analogy between the state and the household. In this relation the sovereign has strictly demarcated functions with respect to the households within the commonwealth.

Hobbes establishes the necessity of sovereign power vested in Civil Law through his argument concerning the state of war that would prevail in its absence. The continuation or reproduction of the state of Civil Society depends on the proper administration of the body politic. The economic processes by which this is effected are described in terms of nutrition (1968, pp. 295–6):

> The Distribution of the Materials of this Nourishment, is the constitution of *Mine*, and *Thine*, and *His*; that is to say, in one word *Propriety*; and belongeth in all kinds of Common-wealth to the Soveraign Power.

The process of distributing the means for the material existence of the society is then associated directly with the distribution of property, such that it is the right distribution of property that will ensure the continued life of the commonwealth. It is stated that this does not only concern the distribution of land, although this is the first law and is entirely at the behest of the sovereign. Skills are also objects of property, and property-holders must transfer that which they can spare in order to sustain themselves. The conditions under which this exchange takes place are under the direction of the sovereign (Hobbes, 1968, p. 299):

> And therefore it belongeth to the Common-wealth, (that is to say, to the Soveraign,) to appoint in what manner, all kinds of contract between Subjects, (as buying, selling, exchanging, borrowing, lending, letting, and taking to hire,) are to be made; and by what words, and signes they shall be understood for valid.

The organisation of the economy is thereby conceived as a branch of the organisation of the polity, and not as a subject of independent enquiry. This is because the question of the distribution of power or property is effectively equivalent to the distribution of the material means of production, the household being the unit of both political and economic existence. While much of the writing of Hobbes and Locke is concerned with the just distribution of property, it would be quite wrong to translate this into a muffled or tentative formulation of an economic theory of distribution. Such a theory is concerned to show how the processes for exchange are regulated and the property of the agents is reproduced. In the writings under consideration here it is the sovereign who determines this process. The circulation of money, for example, is described by Hobbes as going all round the commonwealth and nourishing all its parts and an analogy is made with the circulation of blood. But money is conceived not as the means for the free bargaining of economic agents, but rather as an instrument of state for the organisation of the national economy. Thus Hobbes (1968, p. 301) feels it suffices to describe the 'conduits and wayes' by which this money is conveyed to the public. Public ministers also organise the 'economy' by collecting fines, raising taxes, gathering rents, and in general treating the national economy as a series of revenues and expenditures (Hobbes, 1968, p. 290).

On two counts, then, doubt has been cast on the claims that Macpherson makes for *Leviathan*. First, the political agents constituting the body politic are not the free individuals that are proposed in *The Political Theory of Possessive Individualism*, but are rather heads of households. The economic activity which then underwrites this conception is not between bourgeois individuals, but rather between patriarchal households. Second, the economy of the state is conceived as a vast house-holding process under the regulation of the sovereign. The 'market' between individuals, determining the value of everything and allocating resources, has no place in this argument. Furthermore, the process of economic transactions is not constituted as a terrain distinct from that of politics, for the administration of the state household is simultaneously the regulation of the body politic.

The construction that has been made on Locke is of a different order from that made on Hobbes. The principal feature of Locke's political philosophy is taken by Macpherson to be a theory of individual possession which presupposes the existence of wage-labour; Locke is the theorist of the mode in which the individual establishes possession out of a world held in common. There is an unresolved tension remaining between Locke's recognition of class differentiation and the construction of the argument on property rights from Natural Law, and Macpherson (1962, p. 209) suggests that this deficit flaws the coherence of the political theory. As in the case of Hobbes, the form of reasoning that leads Macpherson to this conclusion is dubious, but rather than confront this directly it is more expedient to consider the argument that Locke constructs.[6]

The conception of property that Locke proposes is heavily dependent on his theory of maker's rights, such that God makes man, and man makes objects, the process of *making* being that which creates the right to the object (1960, p. 311):

> For Men being all the Workmanship of one Omnipotent, and
> infinitely wise Maker; All the Servants of one Sovereign Master, sent
> into the World by his order and about his business, they are his
> Property, whose Workmanship they are, made to last during his, not
> one anothers Pleasure. And being furnished with like Faculties,
> sharing all in one Community of Nature, there cannot be supposed
> any such *Subordination* among us, that may Authorise us to destroy
> one another, as if we were made for one anothers uses, as the inferior
> ranks of Creatures are for ours.

Just as God is the proprietor of man, so man is proprietor of his actions; intentional activity which exercises this property on the materials that God has provided for man's use creates rights of possession in the objects so formed. Furthermore, freedom to exercise this capacity is a necessary part of the preservation of man, such that it is not possible to surrender this capacity voluntarily into the control of a third party. To do so would be to surrender that which is not the property of man, i.e. his life, for this is the property of God.[7] Locke argues that it is lawful to kill any person who would take away this liberty, as, for example, a thief (1960, p. 320), since if a thief seeks to deprive a person of liberty, then there is no guarantee that he will not take everything else, and therefore the thief enters into a state of war with the person concerned. By the same argument, a man cannot enslave himself to another, unless he is captured in a state of war and instead of putting the captive to death the conqueror chooses to make him a slave (Locke, 1960, p. 326).

The chapter 'Of Property' succeeds these arguments, and begins from the problem that while God has given the earth to man in common, it has to be explained how individuals come to have property on the earth. The answer to this problem lies in the property that each man has in his own person (Locke, 1960, pp. 328–9):

> Though the Earth, and all inferior Creatures be common to all Men,
> yet every Man has a *Property* in his own *Person*. This no Body has any
> Right to but himself. The *Labour* of his body, and the *Work* of his
> Hands, we may say, are properly his. Whatsoever then he removes

out of the State that Nature hath provided, and left it in, he hath mixed his *Labour* with, and joyned to it something that is his own, and thereby makes it his *Property*. It being by him removed from the common state Nature placed it in, hath by this *labour* something annexed to it, that excludes the common right of other Men. For this *Labour* being the unquestionable Property of the Labourer, no Man but he can have a right to what that is once joyned to, at least where there is enough, and as good left in common for others.

As Tully points out, (1977, p. 138) this brings us full circle back from the analogy of God bringing the world into being with man bringing intentional actions into being. Just as God is the proprietor of the world which he intentionally brings into existence, so man is 'the proprietor of the intentional actions he makes and the person thus made out of the consciousness of these acts (his "personality")' (1977, p. 139). In addition, it is the rider that Locke adds to the passage cited above that is often ignored when this conception of individuation from the commonality is read as a theory of private property. The condition for the appropriation of resources by the individual is that these should be only sufficient for the subsistence of the individual, and not prejudice by this act the subsistence of other individuals. There are particular circumstances in which this is waived, but it can be registered here that it is not possible to derive from the argument of maker's rights through labour the right of exclusive and unlimited appropriation. (Tully, 1977, p. 171):

> The precondition of appropriation on the common is that there is enough and as good for others. If there is not, then any appropriation is robbery. This precondition is met naturally in the state of nature by the abundance of land and the limited ability of man to exercise his labour.

In the case of land the limit of use is the products that are immediately usable, and not the amount of land that can be used. It is not therefore the capacity to labour of the person which sets the extent of the claim, but the basic needs of the person for subsistence. The appropriation of anything beyond this limit is robbery against fellow men.[8]

The *action* of the person is used by Locke synonymously with the *labour* of the person. It is this action or labour which makes the difference between mine and thine; the intentional action of the person is constitutive of rights of property. Since labour is the form of action, it has been thought that this naturally invalidated possession claims by non-labourers, i.e. landlords and capitalists, and as will be shown in the penultimate chapter, this is precisely what the Ricardian Socialists saw in Locke. On the other hand, certain apparent ambiguities have been identified by Macpherson as the sign of the ambivalence of Locke's argument, and the basis of the arguments can be seen in the following passage (Locke, 1960, p. 330):

> We see in *Commons*, which remain so by Compact, that 'tis the taking any part of what is common, and removing it out of the state Nature leaves it in, which *begins the Property*; without which the Common is of no use. And the taking of this or that part, does not depend on the express consent of all the Commoners. Thus the Grass my Horse has bit; the Turfs my Servant has cut; and the Ore I have digg'd in any place where I have a right to them in common with others, becomes my *Property*, without the assignation or consent of any body. The *labour* that was mine, removing them out of that common state they were in, hath *fixed* my *Property* in them.

The first part of this passage recapitulates the notion that has already been dealt with concerning the mode of just individuation. But the form in which this is illustrated introduces an apparent displacement: far from the direct activity of the subject being the title to property, it seems that Locke assumes that the labour of a servant provides sufficient title to the master of that servant, who assumes the possession of the products of the labour of the servant by virtue of this relation.

This apparent problem does not arise in the case of the ore, for this can clearly be brought under the standard usage of maker's right. But in the case of the servant, the position is not so clear cut. The first point of clarification that must be made is that Locke distinguishes sharply between the state of service and the state of slavery. The position of the servant is therefore not analogous here with that of the slave outlined above. Only a free man can agree to make himself a servant, because a free agent is the only agent capable of making a contract (Tully, 1977, p. 164):

> Since the labour of a person is, by definition, action determined by the will of the person, it is logically impossible for a person to alienate *his* labour. Therefore, Locke carefully writes that the free man (who makes himself a servant) sells to the other free man (who makes himself a master) the 'service' which he undertakes to do. That is, he sells not *his* labour (which is impossible), but rather the service or task which he undertakes to do.

The role of the master is to give the authority to perform the service, but not to direct the servant *how* to do it. The activity of the maker is therefore not directed, and contractually the product of this activity is the possession of the master. In this way the turfs cut by the servant are the mine of the master, despite the fact that he plays no part in the conception and execution of the task which separates these objects out from the common and makes them objects of property. This follows strictly along lines of reasoning present in Natural Law theory, and it is incorrect to suppose that the institution of wage-labour has to be invoked to explain an apparent inconsistency. Note how Macpherson (1962, p. 215) establishes this argument:

> For property in the bourgeois sense is not only a right to enjoy or use; it is a right to dispose of, to exchange, to alienate. To Locke a man's labour is so unquestionably his own property that he may freely sell it for wages. A freeman may sell to another 'for a certain time, the Service he undertakes to do, in exchange for wages he is to receive'. The labour thus sold becomes the property of the buyer, who is then entitled to appropriate the produce of that labour.

It is thus clear that Macpherson believes that the more the capacity to labour is the 'mine' of the labourer, the more he can dispose of it as he wishes. The bourgeois conception of property is thereby considered 'more comprehensive' than earlier conceptions. But as has been shown above, the life of the free man is indubitably his, and belongs to no other; but this does not include power to end that life, for this alone is in the power of God. And this in general has to be emphasised repeatedly when the word 'property' is deployed in modern writing, for it is too easily assumed that earlier forms of the concept, in making strict demarcations concerning alien ability, are more restricted in some way than the 'more general' modern forms. It is apparent that this is precisely the assumption that Macpherson makes here, in treating pre-bourgeois forms of property in labour as 'less developed' than bourgeois forms.

But this problem is compounded in the above passage by a confusion over *what is sold*. It has been shown above that what the servant proposes to the master is to exchange under contract certain defined services. This is 'the Service he undertakes to do'. Macpherson assumes that this refers to the *capacity* to perform this service, rather than the service itself. For Locke this would be to place the servant in the position of the slave, and this, as he states, no free man can do. If we follow Macpherson on this, then the illustration noted above would not need to make any differentiation between the labour of the servant and that of the horse: the ability to labour of them both would be owned in similar fashions, and further both would have to work under the supervision of the master. But Locke introduces the labour of the horse as a distinct category, conceived as analogous to that of the slave. The horse is under the absolute will of the master, and therefore not capable of property; since the horse is not capable of property, it is also not capable of labour. The labour which makes the productions of the horse that of the master is the labour of domesticating and feeding the horse. It is in this way that the labour of the servant and the labour of the horse are conceived by Locke according to two quite distinct models (Tully, 1977, p. 168).

Economic activity is demarcated along these lines also. While the activity of the horse is regulated by the master, the labour of the servant is not. While the objects produced bring the servant into the household economy, it cannot be said that the master of the household directs the activity of the servant in the manner of a capitalist. The conditions under which the labour is performed are embodied in the contract between the parties, and the conditions under which they can contract are determined by the government. The capitalist then on two counts is negated in this form of economic organisation, for he is unemployed both in his own enterprise and as a competitor with others. Thus it is not only wage-labour which is absent from Locke's writings; the capitalist finds no space there either. The economic agents that are constructed in Locke's writings on property are not dependent on capitalist relations for their plausibility, as Macpherson argues; on the contrary, the categories which are there set to work make such relations redundant.

This is not of course to argue that capitalist relations 'did not exist' in the seventeenth century, simply that the discursive demonstration of such relations requires a different kind of discussion from the one conducted here. Such a discussion would not in any case alter the points made with respect to the writings of Hobbes and Locke, since the argument made here does not depend for its validity on the invocation of a form of economy as a support for a particular kind of political theory. It has been possible to show that attempts to trace the presence of capitalist forms of property, and economic agents such as wage-labourer and capitalist, depend on a dislocation of the mode of constituting political and economic agents in Hobbes and Locke. Far from reflecting an emergent capitalist reality, the discourse turns obstinately on a patriarchal form of organisation that had been the currency of 'civil society' since the time of Plato. However, it must be emphasised that this reflection on household and state contains within it the means of assessing the state of economic activity requisite for the continued existence of Civil Society. As has been shown, the conception of particular forms of economic activity were central to the constitution of a polity, while at the same time this form of argument negated the terrain of an economics. Quite how this process of intertwining and simultaneous negation functions can be illustrated by reference to a corpus of literature which directs itself to the management of the crucial sector of the economy for the seventeenth-century: the production of agricultural goods. By considering this body of writing and contrasting it with later eighteenth-century agricultural treatises, it will become more evident that the unities labelled 'seventeenth-century economics' are in fact parasitic on discursive forms that evade such an easy reduction.

4

The Agricultural Treatise
1600–1800

When Harrington constructed his ideal political society in *Oceana* he based the political order on a set of military tenures which depended on the distribution of land among freeholders. However, it should not be assumed that because land is elevated in this fashion into the most crucial economic sector Harrington can either justify this or elaborate on it; as Pocock (1957, p. 128) has pointed out, it would be an error to suppose that a matrix of economic relationships existed for Harrington which could be the means for such an investigation. This argument is supported further if we consider those writings which expressly concerned themselves with this agricultural sector and attempted to advance arguments both as to its prime significance and also concerning the most effective management of it as a resource. Such writing is embodied in the husbandry tracts of the seventeenth century, texts which appear far removed from the lofty considerations of Hobbes and Locke, but which in a curiously displaced fashion carry the notions of patriarchy, household and property into the practical world of the farm and the seasons. Of course there are notable precedents for such a transfer: we have only to turn to Xenophon's *The Economist* (1897, pp. 200, 212 ff., 265 ff.) to find a delineation of 'the house' as the possessions of a man, the description of the wife as manager of the household, and an outline of the tasks of the man in the administration of the crops and agricultural labour. In addition to this Cato's *On Agriculture* carefully records at length the necessary tasks and requirements for the good running of a farm, as does Varro in more celebratory vein. It is within this classical frame that the burgeoning literature on husbandry in the seventeenth-century locates itself, even if at first glance the tracts appear to offer random advice on ploughs, courses and crops in a haphazard and technical exposition.

Until recently these texts have been treated as little more than repositories of facts concerning seventeenth-century farming: the writings address us as if we were seventeenth- or eighteenth-century farmers or landed gentlemen. This mode of reading registers that these texts are indeed archaic, but conceives them principally from the point of view of their recommendations rather than their exposition and structure. They are assembled according to a chronology of writing (Fussell, 1947), of authors (McDonald, 1908), and of farming practice (Ernle, 1961). All these readings establish a continuity in this literature: it is all about farming, possibly eccentric and curious, but of no further interest. It will be shown here, however, that by reading these works as literary products rather than as farming books, some different conclusions can be drawn, conclusions which enable us to measure the discursive space which divides the 'seventeenth' from the 'eighteenth' century. Thus it will be shown later in this chapter how the organisation of eighteenth-century 'agricultural treatises' turns on the organisation of a farm as a productive unit, displacing the seventeenth-century principle of the 'husbandman on his lands'. Such a displacement is dependent on the possibility of constituting an economic terrain, a terrain which under the conditions of the seventeenth-century treatise cannot be formulated.

We can begin by considering the abstract of Estienne's *Maison rustique, or the Countrey Farme* (1606), translated from the French at the turn of the century and after that frequently cited during the seventeenth century as a standard text:

> There is contained in this last edition whatsoever can be required for the building or good ordering of a Husbandmans house or Countrey Farme: as namely to foresee the changes and alterations of times, to know the motions and powers of the Sun and the Moone, upon the things about which Husbandry is occupied, as to cure the sicke labouring man, to cure beasts and flying fowles of all sorts, to dresse, plant or make Gardens as well for the Kitchen and Physique use, as also in quarters, with many fair and cunning portraitures, to make compartments of divers fashions in every quarter: with a large description of the herbe *Nicotiana* or *Petum*, also of the root Mechoacan: to plant, graft, and order Orange trees, Citron trees, and such other strange trees: to order bees: to make Conserves, to preserve fruits, flowers, roots and rindes: to make Hony and Wax: to plant and graft all sorts of fruit trees: to make Cider, Perrie, drink of Ceruises and oiles: to distill waters and oiles, or quintessence of

whatsoever the Husbandmans store and increase, with many paternes
of alembecks for the distilling of them: to feed and preserve
Silkewormes: to make and maintain Medow grounds, Fish ponds of
running and standing waters: to take Fishes: to measure and till
Corne ground: to bake bread: to dresse baked meats: to brew beer: to
trim vines: to make medicinable wines, with a very large and
excellent discourse touching the nature and qualitie of wine in
generall: and after that, another speciall and particular one of all such
wines as grow in *Gasconie, Languedoc, Touraine, Orleans, Paris* and
other countries of France: to plant woods of timber trees and
undergrowth: to make a Warren: to breed Herons: and to imparke
wilde beasts. And lastly in the end a brief discourse of the nature,
manner of taking and feeding of the Nightingale, Linnet, Goldfinch,
Siskin, Larke, and other such singing and melodious birds.

It can be seen from this that husbandry in the quite literal sense is the
concern of such writing: not 'how a farm should be managed' (as is in
certain respects the concern of Cato and Columella), but rather a
specification of how the plants should be cared for and made the objects
of consumption for the husbandman. Such a pattern is also clear from
the earlier text of Fitzherbert, whose *Book of Husbandry* was preserved
in plagiaries throughout the seventeenth-century. In this work it is stated
clearly that the husbandman is central for the organisation of such an
agricultural discourse (1882, p. 1):

> The most generall lyvynge that husbandes can have, is by plowynge
> and sowyng of theyr cornes, and rerynge or bredynge of theyr cattel,
> and not the one withoute the other. Then is the ploughe the most
> necessaryest instrumente that an husbande can occupy. Wherefore it
> is convenyent to be knowen, howe a plough shulde be made.

Here we have a description of the husbandman and his activity, a
recurring image in the literature of the seventeenth century which
continually states and restates advice to an individual on the care of
animals, the ploughing of land, and the sowing of corn.

But in these early writings not only is the work of the husbandman
delineated, but also the tasks allotted to the wife in the household, and as
both Fitzherbert and Tusser, in his *Five Hundreth Pointes of Good
Husbandrie* (1586, p. 13), emphasise, the good ordering of the household
is vital to the well-being of the husbandman as representative of the
household order. However, this mode of description of the agricultural
economy does not permit the constitution of a terrain of economic

activity. The good regulation of agricultural work is conceived as the adequate performance of a householder without reference to the place of this household in a national or even local economy. Indeed, the only extra-household relations which could be considered, those pertaining to landlord and tenant, are not formulated within the strictly agricultural texts, but as we shall see are to be found in legal treatises concerning the relations of a lord to his copyholders and the responsibilities of each. The disjunction between these different levels ensures that the labours of the husbandman cannot be considered as a part of a national economy apart from the crudest aggregative approach to the 'wealth of a nation'. *Husbandry* is the activity of maintaining resources which are given to man by God; any increase in such resources through the activity of the husbandman is his gain or profit, a reward for his personal diligence rather than the outcome of a specified and discrete process of production. The recommendation of cited practices is supported by reference to experience or biblical quotation, in which God is deployed as the prime Being of Nature. Any attempt to provide a more sophisticated version of this form of discourse turns to natural philosophy for its abstractions, producing as the highest 'theoretical' statement within this discursive form an *alchemy of soils*.

The process of agricultural production begins and ends with the activity of the husbandman, an individual divorced from any specific social or economic status, whether yeoman or cottar, owner or tenant. No indication of this ever appears in the writings, and it would be erroneous to assign arbitrarily such a social characterisation to the figures that present themselves in the literature. These figures are not defined in terms of a set of social relationships; rather they are conceived with respect to their activity in the world which God has brought into being. The sole endowment of such an individual is to be charged with the care and tillage of the land (Worlidge, 1675, p. 1):

> The Judicious and Understanding Husbandman must first consider the Subject wheron to spend his Time, Cost, and Labor, viz. The Earth, or Ground; which we usually term either Meadow, Arable, Pasture, Woodland, Orchard, or Garden-ground; then, whether it be more Commodious or Profitable for Meadow, for Pasture, or for Woods, which in most places are naturally produced, to the great advantage of the Husbandman; or with what particular Species of Grain, Pulse, Trees, Fruits, or other Vegetables, it is best to sow or plant the same, to his greatest benefit; and with what Beasts, Fowl, or other Animals, to stock his Farm or other Lands. Also he is to

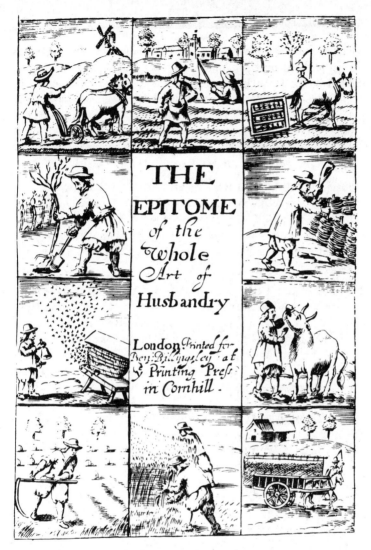

THE

EPITOME

of the

Whole

Art of

Husbandry

London *Printed for*
Benj. Billingsley at
ye Printing Press
in Cornhill.

Figure 1   Frontispiece to Blagrave's *Epitome of the Whole Art of Husbandry*
(1675)

consider the best or most commodious way of Tilling, Improving,
Propagating, Planting, and Manuring all such Meadows, Arable and
Pasture-Lands, Woods, Orchards, and Gardens; and the Reasons and
Causes of such Improvement.

This image of the husbandman in his fields is represented pictorially by
the frontispiece of Blagrave's *Epitome of the Whole Art of Husbandry*,

which summarises the manner in which the agricultural process is conceived as the intervention of man in a natural world (Figure 1). The process of production, from ploughing to sowing to reaping, is conceived as the outcome of the conscious activity of the individual, without whose intervention nothing takes place. 'Production', then, in this conception is a property of man, it is the natural outcome of human activity. The plough is further placed in a privileged position mediating Man and Nature (Worlidge, 1675, p. 31):

> In greatest esteem, and most worthy of our Care, is the Arable Land, yielding unto the Laborious Husbandman the most necessary Sustenation this Life requires, but not without industry and toil; the Plough being the most happy Instrument that ever was discovered; the Inventor of the use whereof was by the Heathens celebrated as a Goddess.

This conception of agriculture as the concern of morality as well as subsistence goes back to the Ancient World that Mossé (1969, p. 37) describes, where work in the fields was regarded as a kind of school for virtue and courage. The implication of the technical concern of good practice in agriculture with a moral concern for the virtuous activity of the individual emerges continually in the seventeenth-century, more noticeable perhaps because of its sudden disappearance in the mid-eighteenth century.

As has been stated, the writings which concern the social relations of this husbandman are not primarily *agrarian* in nature, but rather *legal*, seeking to formulate the relations governed respectively by manorial and customary law, posing the manor as the principal socio-legal institution, and systematising the legitimate spheres of interest for the lord, copyholder, freeholder and steward. For example, Norden's *The Surveior's Dialogue* introduces the category of 'tenant', but the role is construed with respect to a lord who has authority over his tenants by virtue of their enfeoffment, the relation referring in the first instance not to the letting of land but to a state of subservience (1618, p. 5):

> Under the King is every Lord of a Mannor chiefe and head over his Tennants, namely, over such as hold of him: And he hath a kind of commaund and superior power over them, as they are his Tennants, and for that cause he is called, and they doe acknowledge him to be their Lord.

Calthrope's *Relation betweene the Lord of a Mannor and the Coppy-Holder his Tenant* likewise begins the exposition of agrarian relations from the institution of the manor, which is, as has been shown in chapter 2, a purely legal entity and not one which effectively expresses the organisation of the rural economy. The 'tenant' in such writing is thus quite distinct from the 'tenant' that will emerge in the later eighteenth century, for the category here is conceived within a framework of post-feudal law, with concomitant legal and moral obligations, which are partially expressed in the payment of a tribute called 'rent'. The discursive space occupied by the eighteenth-century tenant on the other hand is one which is itself only reproduced by the adoption of the good practices recommended to him by the treatises. If these are fallen short of, the tenant runs the risk of being dispossessed of the land held contractually for the time specified in the lease, thus ceasing to be a tenant. It was stated above that the notion of gain in the seventeenth century was conceived as the reward to the husbandman for diligent labour. This is necessarily complemented by a notion of the land as the source of wealth (Blith, 1652, Dedication to the Nobility and Gentry):

> The Earth is your treasure, in whose bowells are mines of wealth; exercise and suffer all waies of Improvement upon your Lands which are very numerous, draw them to the deepest staple, and there you may easily keep them, but let them not be drawn beyond it.

The earth should be cultivated to the highest degree possible since it is a wealth-yielding treasure endowed upon man by God; effective cultivation of the land is thus a moral and a political duty. God often appears in these treatises as a kind of arbiter of good practice, God *assisting* thought and approving rational activity: 'And if God have made me (instrumentally) Author of a Publick Good, I hope no man will envy that I shall reap some fruits of my own labours' (Hartlib, 1651, p. 6). Writings such as those of Blith are in this period heavily supported by a battery of biblical and classical reference, the validity of the various practices that are recommended being couched in terms of Old Testament homilies or reference to Greek and Roman writers. Combined with this theological principle of verification is the supposition that agriculture is the sole worthy end of man's activities (Speed, 1659, Dedication):

> How excellent and how innocent the art of Husbandry is, has been sufficiently made out by the best of Authors; God himself, who chose out that employment for the best of Creatures, Man, whom he placed in Eden, not only to enjoy, but to labour, without both which no place

can be a Paradise. Perpetual enjoyments without bodily exercise breeding nothing but loathing and diseases; for which cause the actions of body or mind are called Recreations, as carrying on the grand design of God himself.

Such statements are common in the literature, and it is through this, movement from God to man and his activity (considering the proper sphere for its application), that some kind of economy wider than that of the household can appear. However, the comparison with other kinds of activity in the national economy appears only to assert the primacy of the agricultural household in terms of a moral evaluation of man's activity. Meager, in his *Mystery of Husbandry* (1697), argues that while the merchant involved in long-distance trade contributes to the prosperity of the nation, this is produced out of the activity of others. The merchant purchases the labour of others with gold and silver; the husbandman purchases his maintenance through his own industry. The primacy of gains from agriculture over gains from trade are thus established by considering the form of relation of labour to the gains made, and thereby negates any necessity of investigating differential forms of gain in an economy constituted of a number of equivalent sectors.

More sophisticated versions of the treatise, usually directed at the leisured gentry and the aristocracy, attempt to construct a more general argument, but this form of 'generality' turns to Natural Philosophy for the requisite categories. The move away from the purely practical aspects of agriculture leads on to a reflection on the essence of plants and manures, a reflection which could be realised in experiments to investigate the humours of the air or of the earth. The argument characteristically orders itself around the traditional categories of such reflection: earth, air, fire, water. Such narratives present elaborations on this theme while at the same time expounding sound agricultural advice which purports to depend on the philosophy for its validity. Worlidge, for example, employs the notion of a Universal Subject, the Essence of Vegetables, to argue that if a water-meadow is to be irrigated, the water should flow over the surface and not be allowed to stand for long periods in pools. This is sound advice, but the practical reasons (concerned with the deposit of alluvium around the roots of the grass) have very little to do with an Essence of Vegetables. The ideas of Jethro Tull depended in a similar fashion on arguments from Natural Philosophy, but in his case the result was to recommend thoroughly bad practice. The most sophisticated versions then of the seventeenth-century treatise present not a philosophy of labour, nor of property, but of *soil*. Since this is the case, speculation on the nature of soil displaces any consideration of the social system of production which takes place in agriculture, as can be seen from Evelyn's *Terra. A Philosophical Discourse of Earth* (1706).

It has been shown above that the husbandman is not conceived as an agent implicated in a set of social relations, but as a solitary human figure, both in literary and pictorial representation. One example can be found which appears to run against this characterisation: the frontispiece and accompanying explanation to the second edition of Worlidge's *Systema Agricultura* (Figure 2). First, there is the simple matter of the reader's viewpoint – while Blagrave frames a succession of rural images around a husbandman who dominates each image, we are here placed in a position from which we see not a field, nor a farm, but an *estate*. But this estate is precisely constituted by the social relations which, it has been argued, are absent from the seventeenth-century treatises. If we turn to the explanation of the frontispiece, we find that this contention is supported in the juxtaposition of the image of the estate and the explanation of it in terms of the classical argument of the seventeenth century. As soon as the 'Rustick Seat' is noted, the lines move immediately to the crops and buildings. The estate is conceived not as a unity of relations, but rather as an aggregate of technical elements notable only from the point of view of the products made possible. The husbandman appears in the last few lines, immediately placed by the narrative in the network of industry, toil and the gains from labour outlined above. The lengthy account of the various products functions to retain this sudden view over the fields to the church and the village beyond firmly within the anthropology of activity which informs this text as well as all others composed in this period.

The texts which concern themselves with the management of the seventeenth-century rural economy do not therefore establish this object as a sector of a national economy, or even an area in which specific rational principles of organisation are applicable. The process of agricultural production is conceived as the activity of an individual husbandman on the lands pertaining to his household. The category 'production' is thus conceived as the activity of an individual, and 'profit' the outcome of an individual's diligent use of his properties. As such, the conception of house-holding that prevails in this practical literature is clearly related to the manner in which, in the previous chapter, we noted the mode of constituting the economic process in seventeenth-century political theory. Far from the agricultural producer being placed in an economic terrain, we have seen that the relation of the

Figure 2 Frontispiece and Explanation to Worlidge's *Systema Agricultura* (1675)

THE
EXPLANATION
OF THE
Frontiſpiece.

Fᴵʳˢᵗ *caſt your Eye upon a* Ruſtick Seat ,
  Built ſtrong and plain, yet well contriv'd, and neat ;
And ſcituated on a healthy Soyl,
Tielding much Wealth with little coſt or toyl.
Near by it ſtand the Barns, *fram'd to contain*
Enriching ſtores of Hay, Pulſe, Corn *and* Grain ;
With Bartons *large , and places where to feed*
Your Oxen, Cows, Swine, Poultry, *with their breed.*
On th'other ſide, hard by the Houſe, you ſee
The Apiary *for th' induſtrious* Bee.
Walk on a little farther , and behold
A pleaſant Garden *from high Windes and Cold*
Defended (by a ſpreading fruitful Wall,
With Rows of Lime *and* Fir-trees *ſtreight and tall,)*
Full fraught with neceſſary Flow'rs *and* Fruits,
And Natures choiceſt ſorts of Plants *and* Roots.
Beyond the ſame are Crops of Beans *and* Peaſe,
Saffron *and* Liquorice, *or ſuch as theſe ;*
Then Orchards *ſo enrich'd with fruitful ſtore,*
Nature could give (nor they receive) no more :
Each Tree *ſtands bending with the weight it bears,*
Of Cherries *ſome , of* Apples, Plums *and* Pears.
Not far from thence ſee other Walks *and* Rows
Of Cyder-fruits, *near unto which there flows*
A Gliding Stream : *The next place you diſcover,*
Is where St. Foyn, La Lucern, Hops *and* Clover
Are propagated : Near unto thoſe Fields
Stands a large Wood, Maſt, Fewel, Timber *yields.*
In yonder Vale, *hard by the* River, *ſtands*
A Water-Engine , *which the Winde commands*
To fertilize the Meads ; *on th' other ſide*
A Perſian Wheel *is plac't, both large and wide,*
To th' ſame intent : Then do the Fields *appear*
Cloathed with Corn *and* Grain *for th'enſuing Year.*
The Paſtures *ſtockt with* Beaſts, *the* Downs *with* Sheep ;
The Cart, *the* Plough, *and all good order keep :*
Plenty *unto the* Husbandman , *and Gains*
Are his Rewards for's Induſtry and Pains.
  Peruſe *the* Book , *for here you only ſee*
  The following Subjeĉt in Epitome.

landlord to the tenant is conditional upon its conception as a juridical relation, and is not expressed as an economic relation. Consequently it is not possible to raise the problem of the hire of land and the payment of rent as 'economic' issues. Any payment actually proposed is an expression not of an economic relation but of the subordination of the tenant to his landlord.

The early eighteenth-century is marked by an interlude during which the treatises of the preceding century are simply plagiarised, and a greater emphasis is placed on marginal activities like fruit-growing, bee-keeping, and so on. Thus while there appears to be a continuity in the literature of agricultural management, as it appears in catalogues and bibliographies, it is worth noting this apparent divergence from the classical concerns of the previous century with its concentration on arable farming. Mortimer's *Whole Art of Husbandry* presents a straight plagiarism of Blith and Worlidge, rather than the previous custom of reviewing the literature since the Greeks. The same approach can be found in Jacob's *Country Gentleman's Vade Mecum*, where the Preface states that his first move in a consideration of the improvement of Nature was to collect information from the best existing books of husbandry and set it down with his own comments. However, this does not take the form of a simple annexation, for the transfer of the material is controlled by the object of the work which is stated in its title. As a result, only the first ten pages are devoted to arable farming, and Jacob (1717, ch. VI) soon proceeds via the proper treatment of cattle to deer and parks, the price of timber, and household management, to the longest chapter in the book which is 'A Brief Account of Every Thing relating to Gardening, both in Kitchen Gardens, and Gardens of Pleasure; as Soil, Fruit Trees; all sorts of Garden Stuff, Herbs, and Products of Months, Greens, Flowers, Ordering, and Culture etc'.

In some cases the practice of plagiarism is marked clearly in the text; for example, when Bradley's *Complete Body of Husbandry* quotes from Fitzherbert, the passages are printed in the sixteenth-century typeface of the original book, clearly differentiating between the text of Bradley and that of Fitzherbert (1727, pp. 260–7). Initially the older text is used simply to demonstrate that corn and cattle were vital to the life of a farm, and to prove the tradition of the plough. When Bradley comes to enclosure, however, the introduction of Fitzherbert's comments displaces the narrative from its established technical concerns (the manner in which hedges and ditches are best constructed, the way in which to lay out fields) to an unfamiliar set of social relations. While

Bradley assumes that the tenant has a lease and is the major party to be considered in an enclosure settlement, he does not actually consider the parties to the settlement. Fitzherbert is then cited, and he immediately begins talking of things that are absent from the text of Bradley: the relation of lord and tenant, the position of the cottager and the clergyman, and the legal means of dealing with the conflicts of interest and of securing the agreement. The text then reverts to that of Bradley, and the purely technical approach to agricultural management resumes – how to carry out surveys, how to align roads, and so on.

The writings of this period also extensively employ conceptions drawn from Natural Philosophy in their mode of exposition. Laurence's *New System of Agriculture*, for example, devotes the first four chapters to air, earth, fire and water respectively. The treatment of agriculture from the point of view of 'earth' has particular effects of its own: if soil were designated, then there might be the possibility under certain conditions of posing differential fertility as a problem, and moving from there to the business of manuring and draining. On the other hand, if land were designated, it would be possible to move to a discussion of property in land, and thus to rents and their variation.[1] The manner in which the argument is posed prevents the formulation of such problems, and instead we are presented with an evaluation of different philosophies of earth and manure. Such reflections are expressed in Tull's conception of manure and air, and his construction of farm machinery as the realisation of this speculative train of thought. Tull (1733) developed a theory that soil was differentiated by its 'porosity', the greater the number of 'pores' being exposed to the root, the better able was the food of plants (pabulum) to pass into them. This led him into a notion of the two surfaces of the field, the 'internal' and the 'external'; consequently the surface of the 'apparent' (external) field could be enlarged by pulverising it and exposing more of the pores.[2] The function of manure was simply to speed up this process of breaking down the internal surface, and this process could equally well be effected by repeated hoeings and ploughings. Since all plants shared the same food (pabulum) there was nothing to be gained from changing the crops cultivated in any one field from one year to to next (Tull, 1733, p. 103). Thus the fame that Tull achieved for his invention of various forms of agricultural machinery rests on his construction of machinery which would realise the demands of his speculative philosophy of earth, a form of thought which no agriculturalist would take seriously. Instead he was remembered for the conception of drill husbandry, and his devices were recommended up to the end of the century (Anstruther, 1796).

There is then present in the early eighteenth century a shift in the form and mode of exposition of the agricultural treatise, but not one which alters substantially the basic concerns of the earlier texts. Indeed, Bradley translated Xenophon's book in 1727 under the title *The Science of Good Husbandry: or, the Oeconomics of Xenophon, Showing the Method of Ruling and Ordering a Family, and of Managing a Farm to the Best Advantage*, and suggested that since this work had not been generally available in English before it would be of advantage in translation. Around the middle of the eighteenth century, however, a radically new discursive formation begins to dominate writings on agriculture, one which displaces the husbandman in his fields and the households as the principal means of economic organisation. The major concern shifts to the notion of the farm as a process, and the husbandman is no longer the agent charged with the God-given task of using the world to the best advantage. Consider this statement by Arthur Young (1770a, vol. IV, pp. 520–1), one of the principal writers of this new form of agricultural treatise:

> The first point of capital importance, is the product of the soil. From this arises everything else: It is the total, which yields an income to so many ranks of people: It is the foundation, if I may so express myself, whereon the kingdom is built: The riches, income, and population of the state evidently depend on this: Increase the product of the soil, and you inevitably increase the incomes arising from it, you add to the stock of riches, and increase the number of souls dependent on agriculture; all which effects are of the most important kind. These consequences will plainly appear if we attend a moment to the progress of product.
>
> The farmers receive, in the first place, the total of this amount: Out of it they dispense income to the other classes; in rent to the landlords; in the amount of labour to the industrious poor; and in tythes to the clergy. Their other expences, in various instances, maintain many other ranks of people; and the surplus remains for their own profit; not to lay up as *Savings*, but to maintain themselves and their families, in necessaries and superfluities; that is, chiefly in the consumption of manufactures.

Far from the concentration on the activity of an individual, the farmer is in this conception part of a series of exchanges in the economy which combine to effect the circulation of the product. It is in this process of circulation that agriculture is pre-eminent, and not by virtue of the moral worth of the labour performed in agricultural work. 'Profit' here has shifted, for it results not from diligence but rather from the good management of a farming process. There is also the connotation of 'advantage' to the manner in which the term is used. The resemblance to Physiocratic doctrine is quite marked; but it cannot be said that the *Six Months Tour* is a text containing 'economic theory'; rather, it asserts certain principles which enable a comparative analysis of farming practices to be established.

Of course the inauguration of this new mode of writing did not occur all at once and on a particular date. The anonymous *New System of Agriculture*, published in 1755, devotes the first eighty pages to a laborious recapitulation of previous writings on husbandry, attempting to prove that the landed interest should concern itself more with the business of farming, which is described as a noble and profitable occupation. Despite this mode of exposition, it emerges that the argument centres around the business of a farm and the best method of raising incomes from differing types of farm. On the other hand other works display a real continuity, like John Mills's *New and Complete System of Practical Husbandry*, which appearing in the 1760s is firmly established in the classical mould by the frontispiece (Figure 3), the text beginning from Evelyn's (1706) arguments on soil.

One of the principal features of the new writing which appears from the 1750s on is the treatment of landlord and tenant. As we have seen in the previous works, this relation was not in the seventeenth century deemed relevant to the question of the husbandman and his crops. For example, Hale (1758) on the other hand treats enclosure primarily as a matter of the redistribution of property relations between specified classes, instead of the more usual predominant interest in the engineering aspects. In addition to this a definite order of exposition is being established, in which the text begins with the plough, and proceeds to a conception of the farm via a consideration of crop rotations, enclosure, and the capital needed to stock a farm. Examples of this can be found in Hitt's *Treatise of Husbandry on the Improvement of Dry and Barren Lands* and Harte's *Essays on Husbandry*. In certain cases this format is not followed, but when this occurs (as in Clarke's *True Theory and Practice of Husbandry*, which begins with accounts and the recording of transactions) it is usually because the text is addressed to a specific readership. Clarke, for instance, addresses gentlemen farmers who are concerned with regulating the activities of the bailiffs who run the farm for them.

The manner in which these texts present arguments concerning the validity of the practices recommended is remarkably consistent, and only

S.Wale del.   *C.Grignion sculp.*

C. FURIUS CRESINUS *being cited before the Curule Edile & an Assembly of the People, to answer to a charge of Sorcery, founded on his reaping much larger Crops, from his very small spot of Ground. than his Neighbours did from their extensive Fields; produces his strong implements of Husbandry, his well-fed Oxen & a hale young Woman. his Daughter. and, pointing to them. says,* These, Romans! are my Instruments of Witchcraft:—But I cannot here shew you my Labours, Sweats and anxious Cares *PLIN. Nat. Hist. B. XVIII. c.* 6.

Figure 3   Frontispiece to Mills's *Practical Husbandry*, vol. I (1762)

rarely does a Greek or Roman reference disturb their reference to actual experience and the necessity of recording the results of experiments. Arthur Young, who indefatigably produced reams of agricultural experiments in his first few years as a farmer, noted the deficiency of much of the previous work which simply recorded the product and cost from year to year for a particular field. This represents an inadequate systematisation of experience (Young, 1770b, vol. I, p. xv):

> the mistake of composing instructions in consequence of possessing experience, is too common in most subjects: experience is an admirable foundation for every kind of structure; but in agriculture, she must be the structure itself, not the foundation. If one tenth of the books published on this art had consisted only of *record of cases*, agriculture, by this time, would have received the same perfection as medicine.

Young's version of 'systematised experience' as presented in this work appears in the following manner:

> Experiment No. n (Culture, expenses and produce of x acres, field y, date)
> Culture (Description of previous crops, and preparation of the field)
> Expenses (given in labour costs, and cost of seed)
> Produce (presentation of account of sale)

This is then followed by a general reckoning between expenses and produce; that is, between the cost conceived in terms of direct labour cost, and the revenue deriving from the sale of the produce in question. This sum is called 'the profit'. In many of the experiments the quantity of seed sown is not given, but only the cost of sowing it. The implications of this procedure will be examined in the following discussion of calculation and accounting; the principal point that can be noted here is that this mode of presentation is transferred to Young's travel writings, where the absence of comparative experimental control leads him to record the details of expenses and produce of farms encountered along his route.

Writers such as Baker (1764) and Marshall (1778) also produced experiments in a fashion similar to that of Young, although Marshall always despised the manner in which Young transferred this method to his travel writings. Whereas Young went on to produce a series of works which recorded his observations as he travelled through the countryside, Marshall embarked on his 'Rural Economies', living for periods of two years or more in particular districts before he produced a description of its agriculture. Young's method formed of course the basis of the County Reports to the Board of Agriculture, which were duly lambasted for their superficiality by Marshall (1808, pp. xxxii–xxxiii) when he later produced a condensed version of them. The introduction to the *Travels in France* by Young presents a defence of his practice in a discussion of the form in which the results of such tours should best be published. The recounting of day-by-day events (as was Young's practice) had the advantage of allowing the reader to assess the plausibility of the description which would not be possible in a text which simply gave a general outline of a region (Young, 1792, p. 1). The letter or journey form thus presents an effect of realism which is its own guarantee, and can be regarded as the corollary of numerical presentation of evidence. In both of these cases the validity of the text is guaranteed to the reader by means of devices external to the form of narrative: in the case of the journal, the fact that the writer and the subject written of being in correspondence (he is where he writes from, and is therefore to be believed); in the case of numerical examples and experiments, the translation of conditions into numerical terms separates the writer from the evidence that is being presented.

Writings in this period stress repeatedly the importance of keeping records in ledgers, and demonstrate the alleged superiority of this or that system of calculating expenses or profit. Young (1771a, Introduction) advised the farmer as follows:

> It is not long ago since a specimen of accounts was laid before the public, consisting of several books, in imitation of merchant accounts; but I humbly think that too complicated methods should not be recommended, lest the farmer, instead of being enlightened, should be disgusted. The grand object is to keep a ledger, or account for every article in the farm; in which an account should be opened for every field in the farm, or at least for every arable field, and one for all the grass. The farmer should in this book directly, without the intervention of a waste-book or a journal, enter all his expences; but, for doing this, he must take the trouble of dividing his rent to every field, so that the account may be complete, and not have an article for rent alone, unless it be a mere memorandum; and, before he balances his books at the end of the year, it is necessary for him first to cast up the sundry accounts, such as tythe – poor levy – various expences – and divide them in the same manner as rent.

The keeping of *records* rather than *accounts* is therefore recommended, for the latter are inappropriate to the requirements of farm management.

Again and again writers like Young and Marshall emphasise the role of superintendence for the farmer, who by virtue of this can be expected to observe and note the appropriate factors, without the need for elaborate independently functioning accounts.

This was not the case when it came to the management of large agricultural estates, however, and the basic accounting text in the eighteenth-century was the aptly named *Duty of a Steward to his Lord* (Lawrence, 1727), delineating the duties of an estate manager and providing him with a set of model accounts. Laurence (1727, pp. 133 ff.) casts up the aggregated income by source (such as all the manors, all the timber sales) rather than by the actual transactions involved, and their organisation as a 'profit and outgoing' account means that the productivity of discrete units cannot be monitored. In this way the accounts of the estate serve principally as a means of general administration of the revenue; they cannot be employed to identify areas of loss or areas of profit. This structure of accounting is imitated in Clerke's *The Landed Man's Assistant*, and then later by Mordant (1761) and Lawrence (1786).

Calculation is thus installed at several crucial sites within this discursive formation: as the means by which the texts are validated; as the means by which the farmer organises and records his activities; and as the means by which a landlord might control the actions of his estate manager. A numerical principle rules as a form of discursive validation, making it possible to reduce to a descriptive form the organisation of the farm as a production unit. This is in direct contrast to the texts of the seventeenth-century, where the principle of organisation of husbandry and text was a moral/theological one which consistently militated against the conception of a farm as a unit of production comparable with other units. Instead here the form of comparison was between the diligent individuals who tended the resources given by God. Once the farm as a production unit is formulated, arguments concerning the most appropriate size of these enterprises can be conducted. Criticism of the large farm is summarised by Kent (1796, pp. 133–4) as follows:

The complaint against great farms is not of any long standing – the evil (if I may be allowed to call it so) seems to have encreased in proportion to the decline of fairs and pitched markets. If it were the custom for the great farmer, as formerly, to bring his corn to the public market, as is still the case at Uxbridge, Newbury, and some other places, the home districts would never be short of corn; but while the great farmer and miller are allowed to settle large bargains, over a bottle of wine, in a private room, from the exhibition of a mere pocket sample, a country may at any time be kept in the dark, as to the real quantity of corn in it, and little farmers, by this means, must be quite ruined. I wish, therefore, to see fairs encouraged, and public markets revived: the last of which are all reduced, in this country, (as far as relates to corn) to sale by sample only.

Kent advocated the splitting of large farms into smaller ones, not in order that small *owners* might survive, but to give an opportunity for men of small capital to fulfil a role in the structure of production.[3]

The bases according to which farms as units of production were compared tended to concentrate on the factor of labour. Young, for example, in his *Farmer's Letters* (1771b, vol. I, pp. 114–16) concerns himself primarily with the number of hands that different units employ, regarding those that employ a greater number more favourably than those that employ less. The consideration of the farm from the point of view of means of supporting a body of labour follows from the conception of the farm as a production unit, and is applicable no matter how jaundiced the opinion of the writer concerning the disposition to work of agricultural labourers.

Complaints of enclosure at this time were associated with argument centring on the monopolisation of land by the big farmers. This was in turn the pivot of arguments against high prices: that large farmers, being able to hold back their harvested crops until the price had risen, and by driving the producers of dairy goods from the market, tended to inflate prices artificially. The defence of the small unit was usually that the farmer and his family could maintain a closer vigilance over the land, and since they hired no labour there was a saving in expenditure on these smaller units. For example Lewis (1772, p. 7) attacked large farms precisely because on these the farmer and his family 'seldom do more than inspect and direct'. On the other hand, advocates of large farms usually took the view that the surplus that the nation required could only be produced on the larger farms. The defence of small farms as *family* units was essentially a rearguard action in the face of capitalist advance, for lying behind the various criticisms of large farmers is opposition to capitalist farming practice. By the end of the eighteenth-century the Board of Agriculture reporters were unanimous in condemning small farms, while expressing reservations concerning the power of the large farmer (Robertson, 1796, p. 46):

The large farmer can keep back the produce, and raise the price of grain, because he has so large a capital; although to this it has been replied, that a bounty, or low duties on importation, would prevent the evil, and even were the farms never so great, the additional quantity of land brought into tillage and superior cultivation, would call forth an abundance of persons, who, from various motives, would send their produce to market. Large farms, it is also said, place the great farmer at too wide a distance from the labourer, whom he considers as a mere vassal, who, when his activity ceases, becomes a *pauper*; and every article comes through many hands before it reach him, when laying out his money in the village shop.

Robertson (1796, p. 52) considers the proper relative size of farms by constructing an abstract farmer, who is 'the key to the whole'. A series of criteria for the performance of the farmer are listed and these represent so many means of arriving at the idea of the process of production on the farm. The first of these is 'time', the time of the farmer being parcelled out as disposable attention in the working day. The second criterion is that he should not perform any manual labour, the third is the necessity for him to supervise all personally.

Another mode of constituting the farm as a production unit is the obsessive accounts provided by Young of courses, labour costs, working capital per acre, and so on. He presents in his *Rural Oeconomy* an extensive listing of the most profitable proportions for grass and arable farms, with differing capitals available. The long lists of hypothetical compositions present variations based on the notion of the self-regulating production unit, the prices prevailing for the products not being considered as a problem. The process of constructing 'ideal farms' is even more marked in his *Farmer's Guide*, where a large section of the work was devoted to means of disposing of differing quantities of cash (or, as Young calls it, 'capital'). It is worth noting that this amount includes within it both the capital investment in tools and seed, and the cash advanced for the first year, expressed in terms of labour costs until the sale of the first harvest (Young, 1770c, vol. I, ch. 5, XIIIff).

Apart from these ideal farms constructed for the purpose of exposition, Young adopted the same form of organisation when dealing with the farms encountered on his travels. The extract from the 'Six Weeks Tour' gives some idea of how this operated: first, Young notes the soil type, and then the crops. The latter is systematised by breaking it down into a number of courses, with the costs expressed in labour. Again, when Young (1788, vol. IX, pp. 235–6) writes an account of his visit to a friend's farm, he immediately turns to the same apparatus. (See Figures 4 and 5.)

LETTER IV.

I TOOK the *Uxbridge* road to *Oxford-shire*; very flat and unpleasant it is; but the richness of the soil and culture makes amends for the dulness of the country. About *Acton* I observed many crops of peafe and beans drilled, and kept perfectly clean from weeds. This culture, with respect to peafe, I remarked particularly, as several of the crops were young, and yet *supported themselves*, which I have frequently found much wanting, in the cleaning drilled peafe: they are generally so very weak, that they fall into the intervals, so as to interrupt the hoeing, and let weeds rife eafily through them; but some of those young crops flood so upright, that I remarked it with surprize; and on examining them, found a little ridge of moulds drawn up in an exceeding neat manner to their roots, to fupport them. I was particularly attentive to this peace of hufbandry, as I had never feen it perfectly practifed before.

In the neighbourhood of *Hays*, are found two kinds of foil; one very heavy, and the other light turnip-land. The former they ufe chiefly for wheat and beans, but fow them in a courfe peculiar to themfelves; they

Figure 4   Pages from Young's *A Six Weeks Tour*, 3rd ed. (1772)

they fallow for wheat, and after that fow beans; whereas in land ftrong enough to yield thofe crops, beans fhould be the fallow, by means of thorough good cleaning, and wheat fucceed them; which is the practice in the richeft parts of *Effex*. Very few oats or barley are fown in thefe heavy tracts. In the lighter ones their method is, 1. Turnips. 2. Barley. 3. Clover. 4. Wheat; than which none can be better.

LABOUR.

In winter, 1 *s.* 6 *d.* and fmall beer.

In hay-time, 2 *s.* and ditto.

In harveft, 2 *s.* 6 *d.* and ditto, but chiefly by the piece.

Hoeing beans, 3 *s.* to 5 *s.* an acre. This is the cheapeft work they do.

Reaping wheat, 8 *s.*

Mowing grafs, 2 *s.* 6 *d.*

PROVISIONS.

Butter,	- -	8 *d. per* lb.
Beef,	- -	5
Mutton,	- -	5
Veal,	- -	5
Bread,	- -	2

They plough here in general with four horfes, and all in a line; a man to hold the plough, and a very ftout lad to drive, and do one acre a-day. The breed of hogs, the true *Chinefe*, large, broad, and fhort legged, from *London* quite to *Wickham*.

There

ON THE PROFIT OF A FARM.

By the Editor.

BEING lately on a visit to my friend Mr. Ruggles, at Clare, and discoursing with him on the profit of husbandry upon good land, he recurred to his farming books, in which he keeps a regular account of the expence and receipt of his farm. The profit seemed to me to be so great, and at the same time so clearly ascertained, as to leave no doubt upon the mind : I was induced to request his permission to look over the book for the purpose of ascertaining it, annually, as the whole was entered during four years, in one general running account.

His period commenced at Michaelmas 1783, and he entered the farm at Lady-Day, 1784, paying the preceding tenant for what was done between those dates. The farm consists of 146½ acres, exclusive of hedges, ditches, ponds, &c. that is, where the plough and the scythe go. Two acres of it are wood, and 20½ grass.

	£.	s.	d.
The live and dead stock of the farm, taken by appraisement, March 27th, 1784; also manuring, feed, and tillage, paid the outgoing tenant to Lady-Day, 1784, valued by Mr. John Harrison, for Mr. Brice and Mr. Ruggles - - - - -	289	4	0

R 2   Labour,

Figure 5   Pages from Young in *Annals of Agriculture*, vol. 9 (1788)

	£.	s.	d.
Labour, rent, rates, taxes, &c. &c. the second half year, to Michaelmas, 1784 - - -	357	14	7
Total first stock of the farm, or capital employed - - -	646	18	7
Interest of which, at 5 per cent. -	32	6	0
Total expences of all sorts, from Michaelmas, 1784, to Dec. 31, 1787 - - - - - - -	1544	18	10½
Three years interest of capital -	96	18	0
	1641	16	10½
Total receipts to Dec. 31, 1787	2103	13	9¼

Products of the year 1787, by estimate in hand.

19 acres of beans, at 5½ quarters
an acre, 104½

Sold - - 10

94½ qrs. at 28s. *   } 131 12 0

4 acres of pease, 17 qrs. 1 bushel
                  21   9 0
Sold - - - 3 15 0
-----------------17 14 0

42 acres of barley.
24 at 5½ qrs.   132
11 at 3½   38½
 7 at 5   35

205½ at 20s.— 205 10 0

* Since this paper was drawn up, I am informed by Mr. R.
that these beans will be above 6 qrs. from the product threshed.

15 acres

Both these forms of narrative are conditional upon their position in a structure which poses the farm as the site of the combination of superintended wage-labour with land, this combination producing a 'profit' which is the outcome of a productive process and not of individual 'diligence'. But while 'profit' has in this way been divorced from the direct action of a subject, it is construed at the level of the individual farm as unit of production. While the farm is an independent capitalist enterprise, the notion of 'profit' is associated with the revenue to the capitalist farmer, and is not a rate of return on capital invested. As we have seen, the capital invested is 'working capital', which includes cash advances; and further, this 'capital' is still bound up with the persona of the farmer. Thus, as we saw above, we have men of 'great' and 'small' capital.

Rent within this set of texts remains as a residual payment – to the farmer his profit, to the landlord his rent. Each appears as that which remains when the other is deducted. In some instances this was expressed in the doctrine of the 'three rents' which the farm must produce: one for the landlord, one for the tenant, and one for the expenses of the farm (Wedderburn, 1776). Despite this mode of expression, the rent was payable to the landlord not as an instance of servitude, but rather as a payment related to the hire of land, calculable in a given sum per acre, which was the accepted way in the County Reports of comparing the costs of land for different enterprises.

With the rejection of the household as constitutive of the economy, the associated conceptions of profit, capital and production are also subjected to displacement. The 'farm' which appears in eighteenth-century discourse is far removed from the construct of Estienne (1606), in which an enumeration of tasks for the attention of the husbandman suffices to designate the process of agricultural production. The 'farm' constructed in the eighteenth-century literature is a site upon which diverse relations are projected, and which involves specific modes of validation and evidence in the exposition of the practices to be followed. However, the account of the economy provided in such texts is simply descriptive, seeking only to systematise the experience of the various writers into accounts of viable agricultural practice. These lengthy discussions of the agrarian economy depend on the existence of a given number of farms in order for their accounts to have any purchase at all – they are thus restrained within a descriptive account of farming practice, systematised by certain rules of comparison and evidence. It is not enough to speak of profit, capital, production and labour; and the next chapter will demonstrate this in relation to what have been regarded as the 'economists of the eighteenth century'. These writings, it will be argued, are conditional upon an inflation of the household to the level of the national economy, reserving this economy as the domain of a sovereign; and consequently the form of writing which is involved in this discursive space once more escapes the grid of modern economics.

5

The Structure of Political Oeconomy

To state bluntly that 'economics does not exist in the seventeenth century' is to run the risk of meeting a counterfactual rebuttal which simply points to the existence of an economic archive and its authors – Mun, Petty, Child, North and their descendants of the eighteenth century: Cantillon, Hume and Steuart. The continuity in certain 'economic concerns' in the writings of these authors, whether it be with money and specie, trade or wealth, apparently ensures that the presence of such writing in the early seventeenth century suffices to indicate an awakening of economic thought. Indeed, the argument that has been presented in the preceding chapters has rigorously eschewed any reference to these 'economists' while maintaining that economics does not have a space reserved for it in the seventeenth-century order of discourse. So on the one hand it appears that I have maintained that economics does not exist while blandly ignoring the work of the economists which can be discovered in an array of standard histories.

These 'early economists' can only be considered as such under specific conditions, related to the kind of problems in the histories of economics that were outlined in the first chapter. Perhaps the principal condition is that these authors take as their object certain problems of the contemporary economy – but then, as the previous chapter has shown, it is not sufficient to write about the economy to be an economist. Another condition would be that in making their analyses, particular forms of argument are deployed and certain categories, like flow, balance, demand, price, value, and so on, are introduced systematically. But what is rarely considered is the mode in which these texts constitute and evaluate 'the economy'. If this is considered, rather than the simple existence of certain words and arguments which can be read as having some affinity with those of modern economic thought, the status of the work of these 'economists' becomes more problematic. Further, it will begin to be apparent that these 'economists' do not deploy a specifically economic set of arguments and assumptions, but in so far as they have a unity find it in their discussion of problems of state administration, in which the state is conceived as a royal household. Following from this, their major concern is not with growth, development, production, distribution or any of the anachronistic concerns attributed to them: they rather address themselves to the question of circulation within the state, and it is in this category that all questions are contained.

An illuminating discussion of this can be found in Lublinskaya's treatment of Montchrétien's *Traicté de l'oeconomie politique dedié en 1615 au roy et la reyne mère du roy*, which has been treated in modern writing as a general treatise on economic development (Lublinskaya, 1968 pp. 104–5). One recent such exposition which Lublinskaya (1968, p. 106) summarises concludes that Montchrétien's approach to the economic process is based on a voluntarist conception of man and a desire to increase social welfare, and the idea that the industrialisation process is central to economic development. However, this reading of the text can only be produced on condition that the policy of a prince is equated with the modern problem of state economic management. But as Lublinskaya (1968, pp. 107–8) emphasises:

> Montchrétien is convinced that the government should actively influence the economic life of society; princes are mistaken when they suppose that it is something which arranges itself. This is not true, for the art of politics is dependent, even though indirectly, on the economy (*oeconomie*), and proper management of the latter is beneficial both for the state as a whole and for each of its members. Of great importance is a wise distribution of people between different branches and occupations. The king must give every attention and care to the common people (*partie populaire*), by regulating already existing manufactories and establishing new ones, giving encouragement to decaying navigation and reviving declining trade.

The state's role in the management of the economy is conceived in the fashion of the organisation of a royal household, where polity and economy are intricately related; hence Montchrétien's use of the term 'oeconomie politique' to designate the nature of the work that he has written. But this use of *oeconomie* should not be taken as simply an archaic form of the word 'economy' in the way that the spelling of 'roy' in the title can be registered as archaic and nothing more, for it refers itself to the Greek root *oikonomia*, used by Aristotle in contrast to *chrematismos*. This crucial distinction of Greek language separates the effective and thrifty ordering of a household from the business of money-getting and trade. Further, the derivation of *oikonomia* should not be read as 'the laws of household management' in the sense of a precursor of the laws of management of a national economy, for as Singer (1958, p. 38) points out *nomos* refers in this case not so much to 'laws' but to stewardship. Perhaps the most general translation that can be made of the term *oikonomia* is that it covers the wise administration of the household and the maintenance of the objects of administration in their rightful place; just as Xenophon's husband begins by instructing his new wife on the proper place for everything.[1] 'Distribution', then, here means the maintenance of all objects of administration in their proper place, and is quite distinct from the modern economic sense of the term which concerns the allocation of the product to economic agents who are placed not by some prior social order but by their contribution to the process of production. As we shall see later, Steuart considered taxation in the polity precisely from the standpoint of whether it reinforced or disturbed the arrangement of the social order, conceiving the best policy as the one that introduced the least 'vibration' into the relations between classes of persons.

'Polity' and 'economy' are not simply related by Montchrétien's usage: they are put into a quite specific connection which designates the polity as the province of the king and economy as its form of organisation – for example, in the quotation above the wise distribution of persons between different occupations. As was demonstrated in Chapter 3, in this discursive formation the economy can only be formulated as this aspect of the polity, and does not constitute a separate and distinct terrain. 'Oeconomie politique' is therefore a body of knowledge concerned with the just and wise regulation of the royal household, in which economic activity cannot be conceived without the presence of the monarch's guiding presence to place this activity within some ordered framework. In addition to this, the legacy of the Greek usage has another consequence: that trade and business are not necessarily covered within this conception. Far from being the primitive theory of trade and international exchange that is constructed in most of the modern histories of economics, seventeenth-century Political Oeconomy can consider this area of trade and money-getting only from the standpoint of benefit to the royal household, for of themselves such activities are usurious and despicable. Montchrétien's text, for example, has been rendered as a discourse on industrialisation, i.e. on the development of profitable business enterprises. However, Lublinskaya notes that his treatise begins not with manufacture but with agriculture, dealing then with the making of hats and caps, linen, woollen fabrics, silk fabrics, leather articles, printing and glassware, and only after this does he consider metal-working, which is supposedly the key manufacturing process in modernisation. The reason for this apparently random order is that Montchrétien considers the sectors in a hierarchy governed by the utility of the respective objects to the state (Lublinskaya, 1968, p. 110). This state is not the same as the national economy; it is the province of a royal household, in which economic activity must be beneficial to this household in order to be licensed and protected by law.

Steuart's *Inquiry into the Principles of Political Oeconomy* was published 150 years after the text of Montchrétien, but in many ways represents an extension of the same arguments while at the same time attempting to generalise them. Between these two texts lies a body of writing which can be designated as a discourse on Political Oeconomy, conceiving the economy as a system of house-holding, and uniting in these terms the work of Mercantilism, Political Arithmetic, Bullionism and Physiocracy. Steuart's vast rambling book was eclipsed nine years later by the publication of Smith's *Wealth of Nations*, a text which rigorously eschews any recognition of its predecessor, and it is popularly supposed that Steuart and Smith represent respectively the apogee of an obsolete form of analysis and the creation of modern economics. Later in this chapter this assumption will be challenged, but it is justifiable to consider the *Inquiry* as a summary of most of the aspects of Political Oeconomy, opening as it does with a clear statement of the points made in the preceding chapters (Steuart, 1966, vol. I, p. 15):

> Oeconomy, in general, is the art of providing for all the wants of a family, with prudence and frugality. If any thing necessary or useful be found wanting, if any thing provided be lost or misapplied, if any servant, any animal, be supernumery or useless, if any one sick or infirm be neglected, we immediately perceive a want of oeconomy. The object of it, in a private family, is therefore to provide for the nourishment, the other wants, and the employment of every individual. In the first place, for the master, who is the head, and who directs the whole; next for the children, who interest him above all other things; and last for the servants, who being useful to the head, and essential to the well-being of the family, have therefore a title to become an object of the master's care and concern. The whole oeconomy must be directed by the head, who is both lord and steward of the family.

The congruence of this conception of the oeconomy with the

propositions put forward by Bodin and Smith on the nature of the household is startling in its clarity, stressing as it does forms of domination and subordination and the necessary rule of a patriarchal figure for the just ordering of the household. Just as in Filmer, this model is then projected on to the polity (Steuart, 1966, vol. I, pp. 16–17):

> What oeconomy is in a family, political oeconomy is in a state: with these essential differences, however, that in a state there are no servants, all are children: that a family may be formed when and how a man pleases, and he may there establish what plan of oeconomy he thinks fit; but states are found formed, and the *statesman* (this is a general term to signify the legislature and supreme power, according to the form of government) is neither master to establish what oeconomy he pleases, or, in the exercise of his sublime authority, to overturn at will the established laws of it, let him be the most despotic monarch on earth.
>
> The great art therefore of political oeconomy is, first to adapt the different operations of it to the spirit, manners, habits, and customs of the people; and afterwards to model these circumstances so, as to be able to introduce a set of new and more useful institutions.
>
> The principal object of this science is to secure a certain fund of subsistence for all the inhabitants, to obviate every circumstance which may render it precarious; to provide every thing necessary for supplying the wants of the society, and to employ the inhabitants (supposing them to be free men) in such a manner as naturally to create the reciprocal relations and dependencies between them, so as to make their several interests lead them to supply one another with their reciprocal wants.

Note that this delineation provides no theoretical object for the 'science' of Political Oeconomy; rather, it sets out a set of practical branches and areas of administration, which Steuart (1966, vol. I; p. 7) enumerates in the Preface as 'population, agriculture, trade, industry, money, coin, interest, circulation, banks, exchange, public credit, and taxes'. These are simply listed and unordered categories pertinent to state policy, setting side by side institutions, sectors of an economy, and both descriptive and theoretical connections of an economy. These diverse categories take their place within the discourse of Political Oeconomy in order to express certain aspects of its work, while remaining designators of economic spheres rather than concepts which themselves could constitute an economic terrain as a theoretical object. The 'economic terminology' of Political Oeconomy which is deployed in the histories as evidence of the genesis of economic thought thus represents a simple taxonomy of phenomena, and taken individually the terms have no theoretical status.

Political Oeconomy is concerned with the administration of an aggregated polity by a 'sovereign' or 'statesman', whose presence is essential to the discourse in providing a unity which is otherwise dispersed among the instances of the economy or the categories that articulate these instances. This polity can be divided up in a number of ways: for example, by sector (trade, manufacture, agriculture), or by consumption (productive versus unproductive populations). Much of the literature occupies itself with the consideration of the relative merits of such elements from the point of view of their incorporation into the polity and as objects of administration for the statesman. Two principal forms most adequately meet the demands of this discursive formation: taxation and money. The first is the means by which the statesman intervenes to both support and order the 'economy', and the second is the means by which comparisons of the different elements in the polity can be effected via a common standard. This utilisation of money and taxation in turn expresses the conception of an economy purely as a system of circulation of goods and money, in which the 'economic growth' of the modern theorist is in fact augmentation of circulation. Within this discursive topology divergent sectors can be evaluated and argued to be pre-eminent: thus Mercantilism is the name given to those writings which address themselves to the importance of trade, while Physiocracy is the name given to writings which identify agriculture as the prime sector of the economy. The former is in broad terms a consideration of circulation via notions of wealth and trade which subordinates agricultural production; the latter simply reverses these terms and has as its monument Quesnay's *Tableau Economique*, which is the most sophisticated representation of circulation within a polity. For the Physiocrats, agriculture is pre-eminent because it provides an origin for the system of circulation; Mercantilists, on the other hand, did not seek such an origin.

In fact, land and labour appear in Political Oeconomy as alternate origins for the course of circulation, which is then considered with respect to its effectiveness in co-ordinating the polity. For instance Hume (1955, p. 5) conceived land as the original furnisher of a surplus of goods and men which formed the foundation of a class of manufacturers, and accordingly he divided the population into two classes – husbandmen and manufacturers – the latter working up the materials furnished by the former. However, the benefits of such an arrangement are not conceived according to the possibilities for economic advancement *per se*, such that the transfer of resources from agriculture to manufacturing are conceived as the royal road to economic growth; as Hume (1955, p. 11) makes clear, the advantage of possessing a substantial class of manufacturers is that it is 'easy for the public to convert many of these manufacturers into soldiers, and maintain them by that superfluity, which arises from the labour of the farmers'. In this way the judicious distribution of the population by the sovereign enables him to mobilise the maximum strength for conflict with other nations. If a state existed without such manufacturers, then there would be no such quantity of labour that could be released, the nation would be weak − for the 'strength of a nation', which forms a recurring motif in the writings of the seventeenth and eighteenth centuries, is primarily a military (and not economic) conception.

The precedence given to administration of the polity in Political Oeconomy necessitates some means of assessing the effectiveness of different policies which are deployed to strengthen the nation. Political Arithmetic was the first systematic response to this problem (Petty, 1899, vol. I, p. 129)

> Sir Francis Bacon, in his *Advancement of Learning*, hath made a judicious Parallel in many particulars, between the *Body Natural*, and *Body Politick*, and between the arts of preserving both in Health and Strength: And it is as reasonable, that as *Anatomy* is the best foundation of one, so also of the other; and that to practice on the Politick, without knowing the *Symmetry*, *Fabrick*, and *Proportion* of it, is as *casual* as the practice of Old-Woman and Empyrycks.

Here in the *Political Anatomy of Ireland*, published in 1691, Petty provides a set of calculations of population, wealth, taxation, and so on, in the same fashion that Gregory King's 'Scheme of the Income and Expence of the Several Families of England Calculated for the Year 1688' does (Barnett, 1936). It is important to stress that this concentration on a numerical principle for the organisation of an argument does not represent an early flowering of the 'scientific spirit', but rather is the only means available for conceiving the nation as a whole. The presence of the respective classes cannot be registered as a theoretical problem within a scheme of production and distribution; instead the endless calculations of Petty and King project the membership of each class wholesale (i.e. numerically) into the calculations of the strength of a nation. This can perhaps be shown at work in Petty's *Political Arithmetic*, published in 1690.

In chapter I Petty states his main aim as being the demonstration that a small country and a small population may be equivalent in wealth and strength to a large country and a large population. What is of interest here is the manner in which he goes about establishing the nature of this wealth and strength. Major candidates for discussion are the countries of Holland and France, representing the small and large respectively. Considering first the land and its rentals, he moves quickly to shipping, fisheries and trade; the population is then considered from this standpoint, such that 'Husbandmen, Seamen, Soldiers, Artizans and Merchants, are the very Pillars of any Commonwealth.' Seamen, however, combine three of these roles and thus are the most useful element of the population – earning three times as much as the husbandman he is 'in effect three Husbandmen' (Petty, 1899, vol. I, p. 259). Holland's strength, argues Petty, lies in specialising in trade, by this maximising the population of seamen and manufacturers at the expense of husbandmen, for the last are tied to the land and cannot be mobilised in time of war. A parallel argument has already been encountered in Hume, who presents a comparably military assessment of the source of a nation's strength. Of course wars are cited because of the intimate relations between trade and war in the international arena, where the trading capacity of any one nation depended on its ability to dominate particular trade routes and ports. Agriculture then becomes a quite subordinate activity which cannot contribute to this 'public' national economy except by becoming more productive, and providing the subsistence and freeing hands for their employment as manufacturers, the latter sector in time of war possessing thereby an advantageously large pool of 'convertible labour'.

Chapter II is entitled 'That Some Kind of Taxes and Publick Levies, may rather Increase than Diminish the Wealth of the Kingdom', and it involves a discussion of whether certain forms of taxation promote or inhibit specific productive employments. A hierarchy is then established for such productive uses which is organised according to the *perishability* of the goods in question; food is the most perishable since the harvest is consumed annually, followed in ascending order by clothes, furniture, houses, working of mines and fisheries, until the most productive employment (according to this scale of durability) is identified (Petty, 1899, vol. I, p. 269) as:

in bringing *Gold* and *Silver* into the Country: Because those things are not only not perishable, but are esteemed for Wealth at all times, and every where: Whereas other Commodities which are perishable, or whose value depends upon the Fashion; or which are contingently scarce and plentiful, are wealth, but pro hic & nunc, as shall be elsewhere said.

By considering the hierarchy of productive employments according to the perishability of the objects produced, Petty emphasises the centrality of the circulation process to this conception of an economic order, for the more durable a commodity is, the more it can be exchanged, and consequently such an object possesses a higher value. The chapters following this then proceed to identify certain obstacles to the realisation of the advantage of trade.

This preoccupation with circulation as the interior unity of the discourse of Political Oeconomy illuminates one of the popular misconceptions of the Mercantilist position with respect to bullion and wealth. It has often been suggested in the histories that one of the problems of these writings was the confusion of wealth with money, and the consequent preoccupation with accumulating gold rather than the things for which it could be exchanged. But this alleged confusion is a natural outcome of the priority assigned to trade over subsistence agriculture, for the means of increasing trade was to 'invest' in circulation and to ensure that as little as possible of the bullion available leaked into a home economy.[2] From this position 'money' and 'capital' are the same thing. A pile of bullion or money can therefore represent the strength of a nation (with the intermediary links of stimulus to manufacture, and so on), for this accumulation is the means to an increase in trade, a perpetually augmented revolving credit that stimulates the circulation upon which everything else depends (D'avenant, 1771, vol. I, p. 16):

> Trade, as it is now become the strength of the kingdom, by the supply it breeds of seamen, so it is the living fountain from whence we draw all our nourishment; it disperses that blood and spirits through all the members, by which the body politick subsists.
>
>   The price of land, value of rents, and our commodities and manufactures rise and fall, as it goes well or ill with our foreign trade.

Thus in his 1695 *Essay on Ways and Means* D'avenant expresses the centrality of circulation in the polity according to metaphors of the digestion of food and the circulation of the blood, both of which are considered dependent for their sustenance on the trade that the state can drive. To augment this trade was to strengthen the state; an enlarged circulation meant a more powerful position. In the absence of an economic theory of production and distribution, money, capital, labour, or gifts of nature were all categorical equivalents for the stimulation of this process of circulation, and it was only through a consideration of this process that such elements could take their place. This is not to say that any argument at all could be constructed at any time, for this would be a severe misconstrual of the systematicity of the texts produced within this discursive formation. This can be seen from a brief consideration of the manner in which the categories 'taxation' and 'population' are deployed.

When Steuart devotes large sections of his *Principles* to a consideration of the problem of taxation, the form of evaluation that he employs centres on the process of circulation and the necessity for this process to reproduce and not disturb the existing disposition of the social order. Any such disturbance is described as a 'vibration in the balance of wealth,' and this is described in chapter 26 of Book 2 where the minimisation of this vibration is the means of ensuring the encouragement to industry in the subjects of the state. Having outlined the factors which tend to maintain or disturb this balance, Steuart (1966, vol. I, p. 322) concludes:

> Thus we find two different kinds of circulation in a state; one which makes the balance turn, and one which does not. These objects are of no small consequence to be attended to in the right imposition of taxes, as shall, in its proper place, be more fully explained. At present it is sufficient to observe, that the proper time of laying on taxes is at the time of circulation: because the imposition may then be always exactly proportioned to the sum circulating; consequently, to the faculties of the persons severally interested.

This is followed with a consideration of the proper activity of the statesman, whose first task is 'to form to himself a clear and distinct idea of the nature, properties, and effects of circulation' (Steuart 1966, vol. I, p. 323), with the object of maintaining at all times

> a just proportion between the produce of industry, and the quantity of circulating equivalent, in the hands of his subjects, for the purchase of it; that, by a steady and judicious administration, he may have it in his power at all times, either to check prodigality and hurtful luxury, or to extend industry and domestic consumption.

Control over this process of circulation can be exercised in a number of ways, by recoinage, charters, or customs and taxes. It is the last which is the most convenient instrument, and thus the subject of taxation receives a proportionately large share of attention in the writings of Political Oeconomy. In this way it plays a double role: as the means for considering the purpose of the intervention of the statesman, and also with respect to individual taxes evaluating different sectors of the economy. In the first case the general role of taxation can be conceived as the dissipation of 'vibrations' arising in the circulation process which supports the polity, and thus 'good' taxes can be distinguished from 'bad' taxes according to this object.[3] In the second case the discussion of individual taxes and their consequences permits the divergent sectors and subjects of the polity to be represented discursively and assessed according to their contribution to the circulation process which underwrites the political order. 'Taxation' in this case is a mode of forming a national economy discursively; however, it must be noted that the resultant object possesses an order only according to a system of circulation, and by virtue of this retains a dispersed and aggregated status.

The discussion of 'population' in Political Oeconomy is, as suggested, a means of assembling the object of the discourse, it being possible only after this manœuvre to discuss the relative merits of sectors of the population. As D'avenant (1771, p, 73) makes clear, people are in a very real sense the wealth of a nation:

> People are the real strength and riches of a country; we see how important Spain is for wants of inhabitants with their mines of gold & silver, and the best ports and soil in the world; and we see how powerful their numbers make the United Provinces, with bad harbours, and the worst climate on earth. It is perhaps better that a people should want country, than that a country should want people. Where there are but few inhabitants, and a large territory, there is nothing but sloth and poverty; but when great numbers are confined to a narrow compass of ground, necessity puts them upon invention, frugality and industry; which, in a nation, are always recompensed with power and riches.

The person is the sign for the economy, and as such represents forms of economic activity and objects of consumption such as wool, wine, cloth, and so on. However, it would be wrong to interpret this concern with the person as representative of a nation's wealth as the emergence of some labour theory of value. A labour theory of value associates specific qualities of the human person with the existence of the value of an object, a value which is assigned to the person by virtue of the nature of the production of that object. But the well-being of the polity is not directly associated, as we have seen in Steuart, with the nature of production in that polity, but rather with the form of circulation. It is only when the origin for the process of circulation is examined that labour becomes associated with value, and then it is usually displaced by the use of land as the source of value, or, more precisely, Nature as the prime mover of the economy. In fact, between the comprehensiveness of the two theses, God creates man, Nature produces surplus, the conception that man creates value and surplus is neatly affirmed and then denied. And these two theses were the ones that reigned over the discourse of the eighteenth century, the first associated with the name of John Locke and the second with the work of the Physiocrats.

The population does not represent wealth by virtue of the possession by every member of this population of a capacity to labour, completing the thesis 'God produces man' with the notion 'man produces the object'.[4] The population represents wealth because it is possible to divide this population into productive and unproductive employments for the purposes of constructing arguments on the policy to be followed by the statesman. Accordingly Steuart (1966, vol. I, pp. 43, 46ff.) distinguished between two classes in the population: free hands and labourers. In the absence of a conceptual apparatus to formulate problems of production, Political Oeconomy continually projects population *en masse* into its ruminations in order to decide on the distinction of the sheep from the goats. This procedure does result in some rather peculiar collections of employments being considered as of a class. For example, Cantillon distinguishes between the 'prince' and the 'proprietors' on the one hand, and 'undertakers' and 'hired' people on the other. Having provided a long list of all those occupations performed by 'undertakers', the following conclusion is drawn (Cantillon, 1959, p. 55):

> By all these inductions and many others which might be made in a topic relating to all the inhabitants of a State, it may be laid down that except the Prince and the Proprietors of Land, all the Inhabitants of a State are dependent; that they can be divided into two classes, Undertakers and Hired people; and that all the Undertakers are as it were on unfixed wages and the others on fixed wages so long as they receive them though their functions and ranks may be very unequal. The General who has his pay, the Courtier his pension and the Domestic servant who has his wages all fall into this last class. All the rest are Undertakers, whether they set up with a capital to conduct their enterprise, or are Undertakers of their own labour without capital, and they may be regarded as living at uncertainty; the Beggars even and the Robbers are Undertakers of this class.

The consequence of this form of division is that the domestic servant ends up in the same class as the general, and the farmer rubs shoulders with the beggar. Such a demarcation tends to make a nonsense of the requirements of the division of the population, but as is clear from the appropriate chapters in Cantillon's *Essai*, even this rather curious grouping of the population permits the different trades and occupations to be presented and evaluated.

The purpose of the division that Cantillon makes is to enable him to establish forms of exchange between the classes in the process of circulation of the product. As he states, every other class is dependent on the proprietors since if they closed their estates (that is, withdrew their land from production), everyone else would starve. By introducing the category of 'farmer' some order appears, and they are stated as taking two-thirds of the produce of land, one-third for the costs they incur and one-third for profit (Cantillon, 1959, p. 43). This two-thirds enables the subsistence of the rural population *and* the population of the towns – who exchange their products for a subsistence. The remaining third is paid by the farmer to the proprietor and this is in turn distributed in return for rural and urban services performed for the landlord. However, it is not until chapter XIII that the farmers are definitely assigned to a specific class (Cantillon, 1959, pp. 47–9):

> 'The farmer is an undertaker who promises to pay to the Landowner, for his Farm of Land, a fixed sum of money (generally supposed to be equal in value to the third of the produce) without the assurance of the profit he will derive from this enterprise.

The 'profit' of the farmer (which is synonymous with an undifferentiated 'gain') is an income that he receives according to his risk; the landlord on the other hand receives an income as a payment for the use of his land. This division of the population into proprietors and undertakers is then added to by further distinguishing undertakers from hired people, as we have seen above. The basis on which these distinctions are made is not the nature of the production engaged in, even though the classes are identifiable as productive and non-productive components of the polity. Rather these classes are identified as phases of a process of circulation, and in Part II of the *Essai* the 'three rents' notion that has just been outlined becomes the means for conceiving the internal circulation process of the economy, described as the 'mainspring' of circulation in the state (Cantillon, 1959; p. 125). There then follows a discussion of money whose main object is to ascertain how much money is required to effect this circulation (Cantillon, 1959, pp. 139 ff.).

Cantillon suggests that the origin of the process of circulation is in the surplus that is drawn from agricultural activity, although this is nowhere stated clearly and he finishes his text by declaring foreign trade the prime activity in the polity. Nevertheless, as can be seen above, the notion of a rent is placed as central to the order of economic processes, without this rent, however, being treated in any detail. Petty, on the other hand, in his *Treatise of Taxes and Contributions* of 1662 does devote some attention to the character of this category. The result is that the rent which emerges is conceived as a direct return on the produce yielded by Nature (1899, vol. 1 p. 43):

> 'Suppose a man could with his own hands plant a certain scope of Land with Corn, that is, could Digg, or Plough, Harrow, Weed, Reap, Carry home, Thresh, and Winnow so much as the Husbandry of this land requires; and had withal Seed wherewith to save the same. I say, that when this man hath subducted his seed out of the proceed of his Harvest, and also, what himself hath both eaten and given to others in exchange for Clothes, and other Natural necessaries; that the remainder of Corn is the natural and true Rent of the Land for that year; and the *medium* of seven years, or rather of so many years as makes up the Cycle, within which Dearths and Plenties make their revolution, doth give the ordinary Rent of Land in Corn.

The division of the crop into three, and the retention of a third for payment to the landlord, relates the level of the rent to the fertility of the land while at the same time supposing this rent to originate in the powers of Nature. And when Petty (1899, vol. 1, p. 44) later states that 'All things ought to be valued by two natural Denominations, which is Land and Labour', he is simply stressing the *natural* basis of the surplus produced in society. Rent is derivative of land *qua* natural object, and not *qua* relations of property and contract within which this land is inserted. As was shown in Chapter 2, the statement 'land yields a rent' does not necessarily say very much about the economic relations within which this takes place, and for Petty the assumption of the truth of the statement is based on the conception of land as the site of the productive power of nature, thus ensuring that such economic relations are rendered invisible. There is no connection therefore between the 'rent theories' of Petty and Ricardo apart from the fact that certain words can be located as common to both texts. Ricardo is the theorist of capital, forms of commodity exchange and the production and distribution of commodities, and within this framework the question of rent encapsulates the basics of such theoretical work. On the other hand,

Petty conceives the powers of Nature sufficient to project a surplus into a process of circulation which exists only to subsist the polity.

The most coherent agrarian variant of Political Oeconomy is to be found in the work of Quesnay and his disciples, who were termed the 'Economists' or the 'Physiocrats'. Apart from this group's renown following the first tabular representation of circulation within an economy (the *Tableau Economique*), they are perhaps best known for their basic division of society into three social orders: the productive husbandmen, the proprietors of land, and the unproductive (or, as they termed it, 'sterile') manufacturers. For they not only proclaimed that the agricultural sector was pre-eminent, but that labour performed in all other sectors was of no positive value to the polity (Quesnay, 1958, vol. II, p. 496):

> 'The labours of industry do not multiply wealth. ... The labours of agriculture compensate the costs, pay the labour of cultivation, and procure gains for the labourers: and besides this they produce the revenues of landed property. Those who buy the works of industry, pay the expenses, the labour, and the gain of the merchants; but these works do not produce any revenue beyond that.

So, in fact, the artisan is not conceived as entirely unproductive since he does produce his own subsistence. In doing this, however, he destroys what he produces with his own labour, and thus from the point of view of the polity no useful consequences follow from labour so employed.

It is important to note the conception of 'gain' and its relation to the process of circulation that is implicit in the statements like the one above from 'Maximes de Gouvernement Economique'. Steuart (1966, vol. II p. 159) for example, conceived 'profit' as a result of buying and selling, and thus expressed profit in the only way that it can be conceived in the circulation sphere, which is as a simple transactional gain: 'In the price of goods, I consider two things as really existing, and quite different from one another; to wit: the real value of the commodity, and the profit upon alienation.' In the sphere of circulation profit appears as a successive marking-up of the commodity's production cost ('real value') which is continually realised in an act of exchange and which under certain conditions could be accounted for as a process of mutual swindling.[5] And in the quote above it is quite rational to propose that the manufacturer can yield a real (produced) surplus that is not consumed in the subsistence of that same manufacturer; for the circulation process is the economy, and even if labour were elevated to the source of value, any 'labour surplus' would necessarily take the form of mark-ups on exchange between property-holders. The Physiocrats break with these problems because the rigour of their analysis rejects forcefully the account of petty cheating that is the basis of Steuart's notion of profit. To effect such a rejection while working within the system of circulation requires that the manufacturing sector be consigned to sterility, while summoning the natural powers of Nature to provide the necessary source of incremental gain in circulation. 'Profit' is in this way associated with production, rather than circulation, but this production process is a natural one which proceeds with man as its midwife; the fertility of the soil and the capacity of crops to reproduce hands to any man that cares to receive it a gift of God that is disgorged annually.

The economy is thus identical with agricultural production, for it is here that production takes place. As Lüthy (1970, p. 93) argues persuasively:

> 'The economy is the wheatfield or the olive grove, where the fruits ripen under the sun and where God is present as the Giver of all good things, distributing His portion to the cultivator, the lord, and the cleric, according to His justice. Such justice is not that of *Do ut des* because the cultivator himself did not 'make' the fruit, he has merely served it as a humble agent in the accomplishment of the miracle of harvests, and he is not the sole proprieter. Chrematism, on the other hand, is the market where anonymous buyers and sellers face each other and communicate with each other only by means of abstract signs; where possessions are merely merchandise passing from hand to hand representative of the sums of money which they have cost or will bring; where nothing grows, if not the profit of the intermediaries; and where God is no longer present, or at most, present only in the table of laws: a code of commercial morality and honesty, the impersonal 'rule of equity'.

So in this way the focus on the productivity of agricultural life is opposed to the sterility of commercial life in the same way that Aristotle opposed oeconomy to chrematistics. This classical preoccupation with the household economy of the farm in which the patriarch rules by virtue of his being cast in the image of the gods, and in which the yearly cycle of production provides a natural basis for calculation of the wealth of the enterprise, finds itself opposed to the anonymous and Godless ways of commerce. But although the Physiocrats are in this way the last Aristotelians of economics (Lüthy, 1970, p. 92), this does not mean that their agrarian emphasis is associated with a romantic resistance to commercialism and the defence of a bucolic vision of French agriculture.

The whole purpose of their writings was to stress the need for a rapid capitalist advance of French agricultural organisation on the model of eighteenth-century England as a necessary condition for any subsequent commercial development.[6] If trade and manufacture were to dominate, then the parlous state of France's economy could only deteriorate (Lüthy, 1970, p. 158).

The Physiocratic conception of the relation between land and labour restates rigorously the treatment of these categories that can be found in Cantillon and Hume; in the case of the latter, what can be identified as a primitive distinction between necessary and surplus labour is attributed not to the powers of labour, as might be supposed, but rather to the powers of land which produces naturally the surplus which can be circulated annually, (Hume, 1955, p. 11).[7] In his 'On the Labour of Artisans' Quesnay (1958, vol. 1 p. 892) restates this principle quite baldly:[8]

> Thus the origin, the principle of all expense, and of all wealth, is the fertility of the land, whose product can only be multiplied through the products themselves. It provides the advances to the cultivator who fertilises it to make it produce more. The artisan can only contribute by constructing the implements necessary to stir the earth, and in the absence of the artisan the cultivator makes them himself. However important the worker might be, it is necessary that the land produce the advance which he consumes for his subsistence: it is not therefore his labour which produces this subsistence. The consumption of subsistence produces nothing in itself, since this consumption is nothing but an annihilation of the wealth produced in advance by the land.

Earlier on the editors of the work of Quesnay (1958, vol. 1 p. 886) had inserted a footnote referring to a letter that Dupont de Nemours, a survivor of the Physiocratic School, sent to Say in 1815 in which it was emphasised that in the case of production 'God alone is the producer.' Man is the instrument chosen by God to act as the midwife of the fruits bestowed by Nature according to a pre-ordained plan: the production of agricultural commodities is thus naturalised, while the 'production of men' is correspondingly reduced (in this scheme) to the simple role of appropriation. As has been pointed out above, it is possible to render man as a secular God and thereby arrogate the statement of Dupont as the basis of a labour theory of value, in which labour bestows all value by virtue of being cast in the image of God to carry out God's work. But if the Physiocrats had proposed this, then they would not have been able to make the sharp distinction that they did between productive and sterile sectors of the economy. So when 'Mr H' in the essay cited above maintains that to resell with a profit is to produce, 'Mr N' immediately retorts that '*commerce is only an exchange of value for equal value*, and that relative to these values there is neither loss nor gain between the contracting parties' (Quesnay, 1958, vol. I, pp. 896–97).

It is this schema that is captured graphically in the *Tableau Economique*, which is essentially a demonstration of the progress of circulation based on the original advances of agriculture. Quesnay uses the term 'distribution' to describe the circulation of the product between the three classes who are identified on the bases of their differing forms of revenue. Thus the headings of the *Tableau* are the categories of productive expenditure (relating to agriculture) and sterile expenditure (relating to industry) which flank the mediating category 'expenditure of the revenue', which divides an annual revenue between productive and sterile categories (Quesnay, 1972). The explanation which follows the *Tableau* makes it clear that an imprudent distribution between the two categories, which in this case is conceived as a neglect of agriculture and the use of revenue for the luxuries supplied by industry, quickly brings the system of circulation to an impasse. The continued operation of this process is then dependent on the ability of the agricultural sector to furnish the advances on which the rest of the expenditures depend, as well as the responsible allocation of revenues to ensure this. The numerical form of representation permits Quesnay (1972, p. ij) to demonstrate the collapse of the system if too much is expended on industry, concluding that an opulent nation which indulges in excessive luxury in the way of ornamentation can very quickly be overwhelmed by its sumptuousness'. But there is an additional proviso: the return of expenditure to the agricultural sector should not be expected to yield results unless it is clearly grasped that it is to large-scale cultivators that this refers, and not to small *métayers*.

As we shall see below, Quesnay distinguished forms of agricultural enterprise principally with respect to size and techniques of production. The problem with the small-scale share-cropping system is that the poverty of the cultivators compels them to seek the advance of land from a proprietor, and the land is then farmed in order to cover the costs which have thereby been incurred in anticipation of the harvest. Such cultivation is, as Quesnay (1972, p. vi) describes it, 'carried on at the expense of landed property itself, and involves an excessive annual expenditure for the subsistence of the great numbers of men engaged in this type of cultivation, which absorbs almost the whole of the product'.

The principal problem as far as the *Tableau* is concerned is that expenditure from the proprietors on such farms, or more exactly the advancing of land for a share in the crop, tends to equate the sterile and productive sectors; the original advance is no longer in the possession of the farmer as representative of the agricultural sector, but instead becomes the possession of the proprietor. However, this violates the whole object of constructing such an elaborate framework, since the crucial problem of productive versus unproductive employments of revenue disappears.

Lüthy (1970) has argued that the *Tableau* is an expression of the financial problems of the *Ancien Régime*, in which those agents who controlled the allocation of revenues resisted the idea of the royal household infringing on these revenues in the search for sources of taxation. The clear distinction between proprietors of land and cultivators of all descriptions is the basis of the economics of the *Tableau*, and it showed that all these proprietors, including the king, drew their revenue from the same agricultural base. The revenues of the king could only be enlarged at the expense of the aristocracy and this was the rock on which all financial reforms were to break (Lüthy, 1970, pp. 148–9):[9]

> The long quarrel over finances, which was to be a bitter one from 1765 on and which was really a constitutional quarrel, in effect was fought out entirely within this society of co-proprietors of the 'agricultural kingdom' – nobility, clergy, magistracy – on the backs of the 'husbandmen' in whom nothing hinted at a common revolt. The struggle remained outside the other classes, which Quesnay called 'sterile' and which in fact were so with respect to the tax because the royal fiscal apparatus (not to be the last in this case) was in no way equipped to impose or even detect personal or 'monetary' fortunes not manifested in landed property.

The demonstration, therefore, of the necessity for the productive employment of revenue is the means for directing resources into the agricultural sphere, which in turn leads to the development of a healthy basis on which other employments of revenue can be built, and thereby perhaps circumvent the impasse of the economy of the *Ancien Régime*. Although it may not directly appear so, the *Tableau* is in fact advice to the king, extending household science to the kingdom. And central to its recommendations is the necessity for the stimulation of agricultural production along capitalist lines, as in England. But while this might be the material form that the Physiocrats sought to realise, it does not necessarily follow that the analysis that they advanced of agriculture was 'capitalist' in any direct sense.

Meek (1962, pp. 391, 397) has suggested that while their system cannot properly be called capitalist, the exclusive productivity assigned to agriculture and the emphasis on the accumulation of capital qualifies the work as a form of 'feudal capitalism'; and if we examine the index of this text the entry for 'agricultural capitalism' takes us to descriptions by Quesnay of the wealthy farmers of Britain (p. 247). In both cases the designation of 'capitalist' is supplied *post hoc* as it were: the system which Quesnay presents within the formation of Political Oeconomy can be seen in retrospect to be advocating forms of production which were later recognised to be capitalist in character. Similarly the argument that the Physiocrats were advocates of the accumulation of capital depends on the conversion of their conception of 'advances' into the term 'capital'. Of course, as was noted above, the apparent advance from 'Nature' which was the basis of the *Tableau* in fact took the form of capital in the hands of farmers, for in the absence of such capital the cultivators became mere *métayers*. But even if the Physiocrats had used the term 'capital' to describe this, it is important to note that the word in the eighteenth century was synonymous with a person's wealth, and did not uniquely designate a resource capable of being used productively; as was shown in the previous chapter, when Arthur Young used the word 'capital' with respect to the stocking of a farm, this was equivalent to the *cash* held by the farmer.[10]

While it can be argued that the purpose of Physiocracy 'was the advocacy of a state of affairs in which economic activity, particularly in agriculture, would be conducted by wealthy entrepreneurs motivated by a desire for profit' (Meek, 1962, p. 297), this does not necessarily lead to the conclusion that their system was a 'capitalist' one; for the assessment of discursive forms does not rest on the intentions motivating the elements put in play by a set of authors, but must rather address itself to the form in which the arguments are themselves constituted. It would be possible, for example, to argue that the 'reality' that Blith and Worlidge faced in the seventeenth century was a 'capitalist' one, but it is abundantly clear that the writings of these authors could never approach the problem of capitalist enterprise in agriculture, simply because in this case 'production' is a quality of the individual, and is not a category of economic organisation. And so when Quesnay composed his *Encyclopédie* article on 'Farmers' in 1756, the 'capitalist' nature of the economic order that he constructs is questionable. Whereas the writings of the latter eighteenth century in England were quite unequivocal concerning the function and role of a capitalist farmer, Quesnay (1958, vol. II; p. 427) characterises 'farmers' (i.e. large-scale cultivators) as follows:

> Farmers are those who farm and exploit the goods of the countryside, and who obtain the most essential wealth and resources for the maintenance of the State; the employment of the *farmer* is therefore a very important matter in the kingdom, meriting much attention on the part of the government.

Such farmers are not characterised by their occupation in a distinct form of economic order, but rather are distinguished from the small cultivators primarily by the fact that they use horses and not oxen in their activities. It is assumed simply that such a farmer possesses the capital necessary for the advances that are required to farm independently, and the sum required is simply noted with respect to the costs that are incurred (Quesnay, 1958, vol. II, p. 428). As a result of this preoccupation with draught animals, Quesnay (1958, vol. II, pp. 429–33) is led into a discussion of animal husbandry concerning the relative merits of horses over oxen which can, together with the following section on the production of corn and the population of France, perhaps be systematically read as a designation of capitalist techniques and forces of production, but only on condition that certain assumptions are made about French farming. However, it would be easier on this score to translate Arthur Young into a major economic theorist, for the statements that he made concerning ideal forms of production organisation would provide an example more pliant to the demands of such a reading. By opposing rich farmers to peasant share-croppers Quesnay unites two sets of *cultivators* on a plane of equivalence, while one of the crucial differences between them, the use of wage-labour by the farmer, is never cited. In the England to which Quesnay frequently pointed, a wealthy farmer was understood not as a cultivator but as the employer and director of hired hands. In the same way that agricultural production is for Physiocracy the intervention of the powers of Nature, so the engagement of different groups in agriculture is accounted as differing relations to these natural powers. In this naturalisation of the economy (itself the condition of the rigour of Physiocracy) the relations between economic agents can only be dealt with on the plane of a system of circulation, the system which is the discursive condition of existence of all forms of Political Oeconomy.

The analysis of the discursive structure of Political Oeconomy that is presented here is limited to the exposition of leading elements and their illustration by reference to particular writings of the formation. The body of literature that is considered is neither exhaustive, nor given the detailed attention that would be necessary to construct a more satisfactory account. However, the purpose of this investigation is not to provide a detailed account for its own sake, but rather to establish some arguments concerning the nature of economic discourse and the predecessors that have been nominated for it. As can be seen in the case of the Physiocrats, it has been common to regard this set of writings as the forerunner or even founder of economic analysis, a judgment which depends on certain crucial dislocations of the structure of Political Oeconomy in order to be able to claim in this fashion Quesnay for the history of economics. There is, however, a more problematic character that appears within the discourse of Political Oeconomy, a candidate for whom the claims of later economists have proved more fruitful. This candidate, nominated as the founder of economic theory in its 'modern form', is Adam Smith, and the text which he wrote is *The Wealth of Nations*. However, this text is not the unambiguous treatise of neo-classicism that many assume it to be, and in many ways this text is governed by the discourse of Political Oeconomy as much as its despised predecessor, Steuart's *Inquiry into the Principles of Political Oeconomy*. Despite some important shifts and dislocations in the interior of the discursive form, it can be said that Smith's text has only become the foundation of economy theory after its transformation some forty years later by the work of Ricardo, Malthus, Mill and McCulloch. It is instructive, therefore, to present some aspects of this 'standard text', written and rewritten since the early nineteenth century to the present, so that its affiliations with Political Oeconomy can be more clearly located.[11]

At the most superficial level it could be said that the 'modernity' of *The Wealth of Nations* is registered in its rejection of the guiding hand of the statesman and the introduction of the famous 'invisible hand' which rules over the process of production and distribution, allocating resources between agents and stimulating the entire process of economic activity. But consider this appreciation from Dugald Stewart (1811, pp. 81–2) in his memoir on Adam Smith:

> To direct the policy of nations with respect to one most important
> class of its laws, those which form its system of political economy, is
> the great aim of Mr. Smith's *Inquiry*: And he has unquestionably had

the merit of presenting to the world, the most comprehensive and perfect work that has yet appeared, on the general principles of any branch of legislation.

Stewart clearly considers it self-evident that Smith is writing a text of advice to a statesman in the manner of all the other 'economists' of the eighteenth century, and this judgment is shared by the editor of the 1814 edition of *The Wealth of Nations* who remarked that Smith had produced a great work in the tradition of legislation (Buchanan, 1814, p. viii). In fact, while Books I and II can support a neo-classical construction, this is effected only at the cost of ignoring almost completely the existence of three further books, a custom which was established early on in the practice of rewriting Smith, as can be seen in the first French edition (Smith, 1802, p. xxvii), and which is continued to the present in the Penguin edition of the text, which includes Book III only because it is relatively short and the space was available (Smith, 1970, p. 7).

There are passages in Smith's writings which endorse agriculture as the principal sector of the economy in a fashion that is surprisingly clear, considering the stress which is now laid on the industrial concern of *The Wealth of Nations*. Agriculture is described in the *Lectures* as 'of all other arts the most beneficial to society' (Smith, 1896, p. 224), and a passage in *The Wealth of Nations* recalls forcefully the agrarian writings of Political Oeconomy (Smith, 1976, vol. II, p. 363):

> No equal capital puts into motion a greater quantity of productive labour than that of the farmer. Not only his labouring servants, but his labouring cattle, are productive labourers. In agriculture too nature labours along with man; and though her labours cost no expense, its produce has its value, as well as that of the most expensive workmen.

Here we find again the conception that agriculture is distinguished from other production processes by the fact that Nature continually furnishes goods that can be sold but which do not have to be paid for – the productivity and primacy of agricultural activity is thereby related to its position with respect to natural processes. The inflection that is introduced here is that labour is a dominant metaphor, such that the work of Nature is conceived as analogous to the labour of man, rather than entirely separated from it. And this conception of 'labour' and its ramifications is an important departure in *The Wealth of Nations* from some of the more customary usages of Political Oeconomy.

The common principle uniting the individuals in Smith's nation is not a humanistic proclivity to fellow-feeling, nor the fact that these individuals are all human persons – it is instead *labour* which constitutes the wealth of a nation (Smith, 1976, vol. II, p. 10):

> The annual labour of every nation is the fund which originally supplies it with all the necessaries and conveniences of life which it annually consumes, and which consist always, either in the immediate produce of that labour, or in what is purchased with that produce from other nations.

This 'original fund' is one of aggregated human labour, establishing the anthropological basis of the conception of wealth that it founds. Consequently, having stated this in the opening paragraph of the Introduction, Smith turns to the population among which this wealth is divided, and following on from this the proportion of this population engaged in useful labour. The importance of dividing up the population in this fashion soon becomes clear (Smith, 1976, vol. II, p. 11):

> Whatever be the actual state of the skill, dexterity, and judgement with which labour is applied in any nation, the abundance or scantiness of its annual supply must depend, during the continuance of that state, upon the proportion between the number of those who are annually employed in useful labour, and that of those who are not so employed. The number of useful and productive labourers, it will hereafter appear, is every where in proportion to the quantity of capital stock which is employed in setting them to work, and to the particular way in which it is so employed.

The distinction between the productive and unproductive sectors of the economy is therefore deployed to formulate the notion of a nation's 'capital stock'. Unlike the earlier usage of Petty and D'avenant, where the distinction serves to identify useful sectors of employment or forms of income, the notion of a form of labour is used to discriminate among the population of a nation. Smith introduces a conception of capital that is distinct from previous usage – as we have seen in its 'Mercantilist' form this term was identified with the cash invested by a merchant in a trading venture, and in its 'Physiocratic' form it was identified, under the heading of 'annual advances', with the powers of Nature. For Smith, however, productive labour is constitutive of capital stock, such that the wealth of a nation is defined as the productive labour which composes its capital stock. The extensive use made of this distinction between productive and unproductive labour is dictated by the need to formulate a concept of capital that is something other than a simple accumulation of 'wealth' as bullion or goods. The wealth of a nation is its productive labour; to ask of Smith, 'productive of what?' in the way that Marx did later is to misrecognise the strictly limited discursive function that this notion fulfils.

The form in which this 'capital stock' accumulates is expressed in the development of the division of labour, for in order for accumulation to take place the distribution of technical skills, which render forms of labour 'productive', becomes more complex. The advance of wealth, or the accumulation of capital, are registered in the forms of task differentiation that are employed in the production of goods; thus Chapter 3 of Book II is entitled 'Of the Accumulation of Capital, or of Productive and Unproductive Labour'. The examples that Smith (1976, vol. II, Book II, chs. 1–3) advances of this process demonstrate that the distinction of forms of labour in this way limits the notion 'division of labour' to individual enterprises; and indeed the celebrated example of the pin factory concerns the manufacture of products based entirely on handwork, such that it is clear that this division of labour is a division between persons and not inscribed in the organisation of a production process. The conception that 'division of labour' might extend to relations between enterprises, and thereby introduce the forms of competition that regulate the national economy, is absent from Smith's text; as we shall see later, the familiar figure of the statesman is endowed with this role of overall regulation, since nowhere in *The Wealth of Nations* can we find categories which would effectively displace the necessary legislative intervention of this figure. Contemporary economists suppose that the 'invisible hand' is the means by which this is achieved, but this extends only to the wills of conscious subjects who are self-interested economic agents. Enterprises cannot have wills, or rather can only be possessed of wills through their identification with a 'capitalist'. While the capital of a nation is constituted by productive labour embodied in skills possessed by a segment of the population, the regulation of a nation's economic life is effected not by these economic agents but by the intervention of a statesman.

Thus labour occupies a special position within the discursive form of *The Wealth of Nations* whereas land, either as an object of property or as a source of natural powers, occupies no such important position. We have already seen above that the 'powers of Nature' are conceived as labouring along with man, and what is notable about the discussion of rent in Smith is the absence of the conceptions of Land and Nature that have been noted in the earlier writings of Political Oeconomy. The category is introduced as follows (Smith, 1976, vol. II, p. 160):

Rent, considered as the price paid for the use of land, is naturally the highest which the tenant can afford to pay in the actual circumstances of the land. In adjusting the terms of the lease, the landlord endeavours to leave him no greater share of the produce than what is sufficient to keep up the stock from which he furnishes the seed, pays the labour, and purchases and maintains the cattle and other instruments of husbandry, together with the ordinary profits of farming stock in the neighbourhood.

The notion that rent is a simple return on the fertility of land is therefore rejected, and this category is described as a payment to a landlord for the use of land by a farmer. However, the introduction of rent into the narrative is not a device for the discussion of the distribution of revenues between these two classes; rather it is an existing category that warrants some attention because of its relation to the agricultural sector. Further, the statement of Smith (1976, vol. II, p. 161) that rent is the payment for the price of land is quickly qualified by the assertion that this is a monopoly price, 'not at all proportioned to what the landlord may have laid out upon the improvement of the land, or to what he can afford to take; but to what the farmer can afford to give'. Elsewhere, when Smith considers price formation he does not suggest that the cost of the object (its 'natural price') should necessarily correspond to its market price, but when considering the 'price of land' the divergence of the price of land from the costs incurred by its owner is invoked to justify placing land in a special category. Superficially there seems to be no good reason why 'monopoly price' should apply to the price of land and 'market price' to the goods produced by that land.

The distinction, however, is demanded by the fact that the argument which Smith constructs on the level of rent paid makes it clear that the source of rent is located in the product, or more precisely in the price of the product. Having rejected land as the source of rent, Smith goes on to assert that the product is such a source which in many ways simply restores the classical formulation of Political Oeconomy. Later when discussing the different employments of capital, Smith (1976, vol. II, p. 364) states this with exceptional clarity:

This rent may be considered as the produce of those powers of nature, the use of which the landlord lends to the farmer. It is greater or smaller according to the supposed extent of those powers, or in other words, according to the supposed natural or improved fertility of the land. It is the work of nature which remains after deducting or compensating every thing which can be regarded as the work of man.

It is seldom less than a fourth, and frequently more than a third of the whole produce. No equal quantity of productive labour employed in manufactures can ever occasion so great a reproduction. In them nature does nothing; man does all; and the reproduction must always be in proportion to the strength of the agents that occasion it. The capital employed in agriculture, therefore, not only puts into motion a greater quantity of productive labour than any equal capital employed in manufactures, but in proportion too to the quantity of productive labour which it employs, it adds a much greater value to the annual produce of the land and labour of the country, to the real wealth and revenue of its inhabitants. Of all the ways in which a capital can be employed, it is by far the most advantageous to the society.

This version of the relations which put into play rent, farmer, landlord, manufactures and agriculture could under certain conditions be read as a precursor of Ricardian rent theory, hinting in the second sentence at a determinate relation between the fertility of the land (or cost of production) and the level of rent paid. But for Smith rent is a 'gift' which fluctuates according to the chances of individual agreements, and the systematic character of these fluctuations is not a matter of concern. Further, the contracting parties are conceived as individuals for the purpose of this exchange and not as agents in a process of distribution of the product. It is simply the category of rent which has to be accounted for, and as such it is not implicated in a theory of production and distribution. Despite the introduction of the terms 'rent' and 'capital' into the argument of *The Wealth of Nations*; they are not connected in a determined way, but rather serve to reproduce the form of privilege for agriculture that can be found elsewhere in the writings of Political Oeconomy.

Book III of *The Wealth of Nations* is broadly concerned with the historical relation of town and country, and this provides an opportunity to consider at length the sectors of an economy under this geographical form of division. Country can here stand for agriculture; and town represents commerce and trade. The form of analysis is that of a comparative history, in which the evaluation of the sectors is carried out in the guise of an evaluation of the progress of 'opulence' in historically constituted states. While the country is considered the servant of the town and only subject to advance under the stimulus of urban demand, this is seen as an 'unnatural order' (Smith, 1976, vol. II p. 380) characteristic of European states, the natural progression of states being from agriculture to manufacture to commerce. Thus not only is the argument about employment of capitals and the sectors of an economy given a geographical form in Book III, but there is also added to this a historical dimension which completes the demonstration of Books I and II.

Books I and II represent Smith's general reflections on the wealth of nations, but the following Books are necessary to effectively place these reflections. But as the narrative unfolds it becomes increasingly apparent that the 'place' is the discursive formation of Political Oeconomy, and not a formation which breaks new ground. Book IV, 'Of Systems of Political Oeconomy', makes it quite clear that the assessment of Mercantilism and Physiocracy does not presuppose that a new position has already been established; indeed, the only real indicator of some displacement of these discursive forms is not their comparison with a superior system but rather the fact that Smith's criticisms demonstrate his inability to understand the arguments he attacks. The misrepresentations of these two forms are of interest, for such misconstrual does indicate that a rift is opening up in the discourse, a rift that *The Wealth of Nations* at first uneasily bridges, to be later reconstructed on the new terrain established by the Political Economists. The 'Introduction' to Book IV states as clearly as Steuart the foundations of the discourse (Smith, 1976, vol. II, p. 428):

> Political oeconomy, considered as a branch of the science of a statesman or legislator, proposes two distinct objects; first, to provide a plentiful revenue or subsistence for the people, or more properly to enable them to provide such a revenue or subsistence for themselves; and secondly, to supply the state or commonwealth with a revenue sufficient for the publick services. It proposes to enrich both the people and the sovereign.

In dividing up all previous writing into two schools, Smith curiously replicates the Aristotelian distinction between agriculture and commerce, while in his qualified praise of Physiocracy and his condemnation of Mercantilism this quality is further underlined. This is perhaps only a formal similarity, but it is worth noting in the light of the curious manner in which he misconstrues Physiocracy.

Beginning with a remark that in response to the over-emphasis on commerce and the town, the Physiocrats over-react in the opposite direction (Smith, 1976, vol. III, p. 664), Smith proceeds to give an outline of the salient features of their work. He concludes by stating that while the majority of their proposals are correct, the consignment of manufacturers to the 'sterile' class is a gross error (Smith 1976, vol. II

p. 674); and he appends a series of points which support his contention. What is significant about these points is that they argue on the basis of the general productivity of *labour*, suggesting for example, that since Quesnay admits that the artisan reproduces his own subsistence, then he cannot possibly be held unproductive. As has been shown above, the logic of designating manufacturers 'unproductive' or sterile is in the circuit of the *Tableau*, quite in order; Smith's criticisms, however, ignore this organisation of analysis and instead introduce his conception of productivity based not on the system of circulation but on the forms of labour. In doing this he undermines the coherence of the Physiocratic position and reduces it to a simple classical pastoral theory.

In the case of the set of writings that Smith chooses to call Mercantilist, a similar displacement takes place. The principal reason for his rejection of these doctrines is that in erecting a legislative apparatus, states prevent the effective flow of trade and commerce that would result if free-trade policies were followed. But one of the major points in his criticism is the contention that Mercantilism confused wealth with money or bullion (Smith 1976, vol. II p. 449), and this simply initiates a popular misconception that has remained to this day. As was suggested earlier in this chapter, the apparent association of wealth and money is discursively possible in Political Oeconomy because in the case of trade conceived from the point of circulation this association is valid. Having departed from the notion of circulation as central to the organisation of his narrative, Smith is consequently baffled when faced with texts that treat their problems uniquely from this standpoint. The criticisms that Smith makes of Political Oeconomy do not therefore indicate that he has departed from this matrix and can criticise from an established external position, for while in this case circulation had disappeared from *The Wealth of Nations* as a principle of organisation, it cannot be said that any serious alternative candidate exists for this crucial discursive function. Having dispensed with one principle of organisation, there exist only the notions of labour and the 'invisible hand' as possibilities – but both of these are in fact overridden by the appearance in the final Book of the 'statesman', diminished in stature perhaps but with a crucial function none the less.

The role of this statesman is to introduce the legislation which will promote free exchange between states. What is absent, however, is a set of principles that would comprehend the forms of competition arising from this, and thus the statesman is discursively necessary for the fulfilment of this role. Once posited at the end of Book IV, Book V then concerns itself with the forms of expenditure devolving on the statesman, and the means of raising the revenue sufficient to support such expense; a great deal of space is therefore given over to the problem of taxation. The evaluation of forms of taxation is concerned with the problem of the justice of forms of taxation with respect to the individuals in a polity; the following discussion with the different varieties of tax enables the situation of these individuals to be reviewed. In this fashion Smith deals with the different areas of the polity without utilising the device of circulation, and in this way renders the treatment of the polity less comprehensible than authors such as Steuart. Whereas the principles which organised such analysis of the polity were recognisable as an attempt to evaluate the components of economic activity in a national economy, for Smith his concentration on the individual agents renders these lengthy concluding passages of his work abstruse and forgettable. It is perhaps no wonder that this is the fate in fact cast upon them by modern writers.

Smith occupies an ambiguous position with respect to the structure of Political Oeconomy, for while much of the analysis of *The Wealth of Nations* works within its principles, by removing the crucial category of circulation some disarray is brought into the presentation of the argument. This chapter has attempted to introduce some leading elements of this discursive formation called Political Oeconomy, and show that attempts to read out of the texts of the seventeenth and eighteenth centuries 'anticipations' of economic analysis distort and misconstrue the significance of such texts. However, to claim Smith as the founder of economic thought necessitates such work, and in the next chapter it will be shown how such a project was essential to the constitution of economic discourse.

6

The Formation of Economic Discourse

To the end of the eighteenth century *The Wealth of Nations* steadily gained a reputation as the major statement of Political Oeconomy, although meeting relatively few published discussions or criticisms. In fact the spate of texts discussing economic issues that Smith drew on came to a halt with the publication of his book, and it could be said that *The Wealth of Nations* became a standard text through simple lack of competition. It was not until the early years of the nineteenth century that there was a gradual resumption of publication, and when this occurred it could be noticed that the terms of argument and criticism had been subtly shifted from those customary in the earlier writings of the eighteenth century. What was of particular importance at this time, however, was that it was the Physiocratic tendency within Smith's work that attracted the majority of comment, as this example from the second number of *Edinburgh Review* shows (Horner, 1803, p. 447):

> We intend to show, that, in the celebrated treatise of Dr. Smith, though that author denies the ultimate incidence of taxes upon land, the principles which he has established involve this conclusion. That Smith did not precisely distinguish the real import of the economical system, is now confessed, we believe, even by those who agree with him in rejecting it. We are further satisfied that he derived a much larger portion of his reasonings from them, than he himself perhaps recollected; that his principles on the formation and distribution of national riches approached more nearly to those of Quesnai, than he was himself aware; and that, to have recognised an entire coincidence, it was only necessary for him to have followed out his analysis a few steps further.

We have seen in the previous chapter that the argument that Smith used against Physiocracy did not involve a rejection of the agrarian origin for circulation as such, for elsewhere in *The Wealth of Nations* he proposed a similar schema; the objection that he made to the designation of manufacturers as 'sterile' was based on the conception of 'labour' that was crucial to his argument. This conception was developed in such a fashion, however, that it was relatively easy to immobilise its effectiveness and thus convert Smith into a Physiocrat, in the way that Horner suggests here. It was this operation that was performed by many of the writers of this period, such as Gray, Wakefield and Spence; and it can be said with some justice that the first constitution of Smith was as a Physiocrat.[1] Of course this is quite distinct from the image of Smith that is presented today, for as the 'founder of modern economics' he is the theorist of a free market economy, the promoter of industrialisation and economic growth, and a theorist of capital and labour; but this image is also distinct from the one fashioned by the Classical Economists of the next two decades, as will be shown below.

For example, when, William Spence, in his *Britain Independent of Commerce* of 1808, divided political economists investigating the source of wealth into two groups, he placed Smith with the agricultural writers (Spence, 1822, p. 8). Spence then went on to argue that the Physiocratic denigration of manufacture was erroneous, and that in fact manufacture was vital to stimulate agricultural production. However, national wealth was dependent on these two sectors only, and as the title suggests Britain could dispense entirely with her foreign trade and base her wealth on the employment of her resources in manufacture and agriculture only (Spence, 1822, pp. 60, 71). The argument that Spence constructs is based on the evaluation of sectors of an economy as contributors to national wealth, an argument which is a customary one in Political Oeconomy and which does not rely on the assessment of forms of labour for it to be effective. However, James Mill's response to Spence was to argue precisely on the ground of Smith's criticisms of the Physiocrats, and he converted this direct evaluation of *sectors* into an evaluation of *labour*. Mill (1966, pp. 94–5) agreed with Spence only in so far as 'Of all species of labour, that which is bestowed upon the soil, is in general rewarded by the most abundant product', and Torrens (1808, pp. 4–6) in his *Economists Refuted* maintained that it was labour that created wealth, either by appropriation, preparation, or augmenting the productions of land and water. In this way Mill and Spence begin the establishment of a new Smithian orthodoxy which identified the productivity of labour, not of Nature, as the source of wealth, an 'orthodoxy' which in some instances was to convert the distinction of labour by employment that Smith made a philosophy of the unique powers of human labour.

It was in this way that *The Wealth of Nations* could become a standard text utilised by opposing theorists. Boileau, for example, published in 1811 an *Introduction to the Study of Political Economy*, a book which is derivative of *The Wealth of Nations*, but which identifies both nature and labour as the joint sources of wealth (Boileau, 1811, p. 10). In addition the later text of Purves entitled *All Classes Productive of National Wealth* argues that since every person is a circulator of wealth, each person is productive of wealth (Purves, 1817, ch. IV). Both Boileau and Purves conceive wealth not as the strength of a nation, but as rather the well-being of persons, a slide from nation to human being that is made possible by Smith defining the wealth of a nation in terms of the accumulation of productive labour. By suppressing this qualification of 'productiveness' it was possible to convert much of Smith's text into an exposition of the powers of human labour – thus while Lauderdale (1804, pp. 37) rejected Smith's use of labour as a measure of value on the grounds that the productive/unproductive distinction undermined it, he was able to then redefine value as related to men's desires. The unique powers of labour and the universality of human desire became in this way connected as the basis for a philosophical anthropology of labour which conceived an economy as an aggregate of subjects striving to satisfy their wants, and in this way forming themselves into two fluid and exchanging groups, consumers and producers, or demanders and suppliers. However, this humanist conception of the economy did not form a significant element in the constitution of an economic discourse, and played little part in the debates of the following two decades.

It should not be assumed that the presence of *The Wealth of Nations* immediately obliterated the earlier texts of the eighteenth century – when Daniel Wakefield published his *Essay upon Political Oeconomy; being an Inquiry into the Truth of the Two Positions of the French Oeconomists; that Labour Employed in Manufacture is Unproductive; and that all Taxes Ultimately Fall Upon, or Settle in the Surplus Produce of Land* in 1799, he stated quite clearly that it was Steuart who was the great master in 'political science' (as he termed it), of whom Smith was an inferior popular copy (Wakefield, 1804, p. 3). Accordingly the discussion of prices and distribution that Wakefield (1804, p. 33) gives follows closely on that of Steuart, conceiving the grand object as a diminution of the 'vibrations' between the classes. But this is a fairly isolated example, and its presence only serves to underline the dominance of *The Wealth of Nations* in discussions of economic affairs in the early nineteenth century. However, it would be wrong to suppose that the simple presence of this text itself registered the formation of an economic discourse; as can be seen, the writings of Spence, Horner and Gray re-established the text in the regularities of Political Oeconomy, while others carried through a reading which re-established the moral discourse from which Smith had begun. If we are to assign a date to the formation of economic discourse, a procedure itself as regressive as conceiving economic theory as the creation of specific authors, then it can only be 1815 and the discussions around the Corn Laws. And in these discussions of rent and the distribution of the product between economic classes, the work of Smith can be registered only by noting the absence of the problems formulated here from *The Wealth of Nations*.

It would also be wrong, however, to draw from this the conclusion that a specific political issue, a debate around economic legislation, is the 'real origin' of economic discourse. Such a conclusion is of course easy and tempting, since it associates a particular body of theory with political issues in which distinct interests are at stake; nothing would be easier than to argue that the political interests of the time find their clear expression in the new economic theory of the early nineteenth century, that Ricardo is the spokesman of the rising bourgeoisie and Malthus the defender of the privileges of the landed aristocracy. A discursive order cannot be expressive of a non-discursive order; economic discourse does not represent the economy and its conflicts in the sense that it simply transposes elements from one and expresses them in the terms of the other. To argue that this is the case necessitates the ascription of transcendental creative powers to the human subject as constitutive author, the rendering of man the writer in the image of God the maker. Moreover, the attempt to provide some such final causality, the relation of dependency between thought and being, involves the idea that to *explain* is to identify *origins*. In this sense there is no origin for economic discourse, there is no beginning and no end, in time or in space. To begin to understand quite what constitutes such discourse does not require such investigations – it is only necessary to know that under certain conditions it is not, and that under other conditions it is. Discourse then has no history, for any history requires the construction of a chronology, which immediately imposes beginnings, middles and ends. It has been argued at length in the preceding chapters, for example, that to write on the agrarian economy does not necessarily indicate that a discourse arises that specifies this economy; neither is it sufficent to concern oneself with the economy as a whole. If we consider a particular text like *The Wealth of Nations*, it can be shown that it only becomes an economic treatise under certain readings, and that this text does not have a history *qua* economic treatise until some forty years after its first publication.

If '1815' is nominated as the date on which economic discourse is fully constituted, it is easy to make the kind of associations between the political issues and the economic judgments embodied in the pamphlets of the time. But to do this is to misrecognise the specificity of the forms of argument that are made possible in this new discursive form, diverting attention from the novel concepts and arguments of these pamphlets to the persons who happen to be their authors. This can be demonstrated by considering the work of Ricardo prior to the date of 1815, when his *Essay on Profits* appeared; and what is notable is that while Ricardo's economic writings begin with the Bullion Controversy of 1809–10, the issues which are involved in this political debate did not give occasion to the development of specific forms of argument for their solution. Of course this is partly to do with the nature of the problems dealt with : the question of the value of the currency had been a periodically recurring one in the previous two centuries, and as has been shown in the preceding chapter Political Oeconomy was especially suited to providing the means for such discussions. The classical form of the problem was stated by Ricardo (1951, vol. III, p. 15) in his article 'The Price of Gold' published in the *Morning Chronicle* in August 1809 :

> The present high market price above the mint price of gold, appears to have engrossed a great portion of the attention of the public ; but they do not seem to be sufficiently impressed with the importance of the subject, nor of the disastrous consequences which may attend the further depreciation of paper. I am anxious, whilst there is yet time, that we should retrace our steps and restore the currency to that healthful state which so long existed in this country, and the departure from which is pregnant with present evil and future ruin.

The question of the deviation of the prices of paper from gold currency involves considering circulation and exchange in an economy, and the instruments by which this is effected, such as banks and commodity exchanges. While it is clear that different sections of the economy are affected in distinct ways by the problem of depreciation, it does not seem necessary to consider problems and distribution. However, in his later pamphlet *The High Price of Bullion*, published in 1810, Ricardo states quite clearly that gold and silver are commodities like any other, a conception that was to be misunderstood by Malthus in his first letter to Ricardo (Malthus to Ricardo, 16 June 1811 ; Letter 8, Ricardo, 1952, vol. VI, p. 21) :

Gold and silver, like other commodities, have an intrinsic value,
which is not arbitrary, but is dependent on their scarcity, the quantity
of labour bestowed in procuring them, and the value of the capital
employed in the mines which produce them.

'The quality of utility, beauty, and scarcity,' says Dr. Smith, 'are the
original foundation of the high price of those metals, or of the great
quantity of other goods for which they can every where be
exchanged. This value was antecedent to, and independent of their
being employed as coin, and was the quality which fitted them for that
employment' (Ricardo, 1951, vol. III, pp. 52–3).

While the value of bullion is related to a list of factors, and is not
unilaterally attributed to any one of them, the nature of the three factors
is interesting. 'Scarcity' was a general way of accounting for the
constitution of an economic object with value – as we will see below, it
was this conception of scarcity which was used to argue that land was
scarce and therefore had a value, while air and water were abundant and
consequently were of no economic value. In any case this is hardly of the
same importance as the next factor, the labour bestowed on an object,
since it can under certain conditions be simply subsumed under this case.
If this is allowed, then the value of bullion, *qua* commodity, is related to
the capital and labour embodied. However, these terms are not subjected
to any kind of theorisation. Instead this statement is followed by a
quotation from Smith (*The Wealth of Nations*, Book. I, ch. 11), which is
presumably included as a discursive support. What is striking, however,
is that the quotation from Smith does not support the position of
Ricardo, but rather simply follows it with an alternative: capital and
labour are not equivalent terms for utility, beauty and scarcity. So while
Ricardo invokes *The Wealth of Nations* as a support here, the terms of
his own statement are quite distinct from the one on which he calls for
support.

It should not be assumed, however, that this discrepancy indicates
that Ricardo is already a 'Ricardian'; elsewhere we find Ricardo using
the term 'capital' in the customary sense of 'Wealth of a nation' (Ricardo
to Mill, 1 January 1811; Letter 5, Ricardo 1952, vol. VI, pp. 16–17). In
his writings on currency the use of terms which were later to carry the
structure of Classical Political Economy have no such systematic
connection; and while in the example given above Ricardo uses the
words 'capital' and 'labour' as constitutive of value, this should not be
read as an anticipation of Classical thought. Concerned as it is with
circulation, and the discrepancies arising in the process of the circulation

of money, the Bullion Controversy of 1809–10 did not, and could not, provoke the formulation of new arguments and modes of proof. This was not the case with the Corn Law debate of five years later.

In the eighteenth century the effects of the Corn Laws on the price of grains, and in particular on the staple, wheat, had periodically given rise to rashes of pamphlets and tracts, and in many cases provoked local rioting. The publication of the pamphlets was usually timed to coincide with debates in Parliament, and in the case of the crisis of 1815 this pattern was simply repeated; there was a difference in terms of the effects of legislation, however, for it was low rather than high prices which troubled particular interests. The harvests of 1813 and 1814 had been good, leading to a steady fall from the very high prices that had prevailed in the previous years. This fall was not only the result of abundant harvests, it was also the result of an extension of cultivation under the stimulus of the high prices. The peace of March 1814 further accelerated this downward trend, and this exacerbated an already poor situation for farmers who had entered holdings at the point of high rents, and were now unable to pay these rents because of the collapse of their revenues.[2] The Committee on the Corn Trade met to discuss the problems which had arisen in the agricultural sector, and the Report of this Committee was debated in Parliament in February 1815, a new Corn Law being passed on 10 March 1815. Coinciding with this parliamentary debate came the publication in rapid succession of four pamphlets. These pamphlets (by West, Malthus, Ricardo and Torrens) were, however, quite different from their counterparts in previous crises: suddenly the form in which labour, capital, production, profit, land and rent were organised took on a completely new form in which novel arguments concerning the production and distribution of wealth were presented for the first time. The possibility of constructing such arguments registers the formation of an economic discourse, the establishment of a theoretical terrain that had no prior existence. However, it would be quite incorrect to suppose that this represents the formation of 'modern economics' – as will become apparent, the commodity economy which was constructed first by the Classical Political Economists was a specifically agrarian one in which the conceptions of time and capital were conceived according to the exigencies of agricultural capitalist production. This does not mean in turn that Classical Political Economy is a 'reflection' of a contemporary economic form, for as we have seen with the Physiocrats an account of 'capitalist production in agriculture' does not necessitate the theorisation of a commodity economy. For them, land was the source of advances because it embodied the powers of Nature. For the Classical Economists, land was a form of capital, and capital was defined independently of conceptions of the unique powers of land or labour.

The food riots of the eighteenth century[3] expressed a conception of the economy as a system of circulation, the 'house-holding' notion of Political Oeconomy. 'Abnormal profits' could only be conceived as the result of extortion, and naturally those concerned with the distribution of corn were immediately identified as the culprits who were 'holding the people to ransom'. The apparently excessive profits of the merchant were seen as the result of a position of dominance in which he as an individual appeared to the individuals with whom he dealt; the profit made by such a merchant was not related to the stock he held but rather to his monopoly position in a market.

The first statement to break with this established form of argument was a pamphlet published by Malthus in 1800 entitled *An Investigation of the Cause of the Present High Price of Provisions*. He stated clearly that such accusations of extortion directed at merchants were misplaced, and that instead of condemning the person who bought and sold the corn, it would be more appropriate to consider the effect of the system of parish poor relief on the price of corn. It would be all too easy to dismiss the conclusions that Malthus drew as simple reactionary ideology, expressive of his contempt for the sufferings of the poor whose principal source of food was wheaten bread; such an attitude would misjudge the significance of the propositions that Malthus puts forward. He takes as his example the 1799 harvest and the misery consequent on it (Malthus, 1970b, pp. 11–12).

The system of poor laws, and parish allowances, in this country and I will add, to their honour, the humanity and generosity of the higher and middle classes of society, naturally and necessarily altered this state of things. The poor complained to the justices that their wages would not enable them to supply their families in the single article of bread. The justices very humanely, and I am far from saying improperly, listened to their complaints, inquired what was the smallest sum on which they could support their families, at the then price of wheat, and gave an order of relief on the parish accordingly. The poor were now enabled, for a short time, to purchase nearly their usual quantity of flour; but the stock in the country was not sufficient, even with the prospect of importation, to allow of the usual distribution to all its members. The crop was consuming too fast. Every market day the demand exceeded the supply; and those whose business it was to judge on these subjects, felt convinced, that in a month or two the scarcity would be greater than it was at that time. Those who were able, therefore, kept back their corn. In so doing, they undoubtedly consulted their own interest; but they, as undoubtedly, whether with the intention or not is of no consequence, consulted the interest of the state: for, if they had not kept it back, too much would have been consumed, and there would have been a famine instead of a scarcity at the end of the year.

The high price of corn is then related by Malthus not to a conception of individual gains, but rather to the exigencies of distributing a produced good through time, in this case the distribution of the product of the harvest of one year throughout the following year. Malthus is therefore able to show that the merchants, by following their own interests, conform to, and are subordinated by, a distribution mechanism; it can then be demonstrated that far from alleviating distress, parish relief actually contributes to it by driving prices yet higher. Hence, the annually produced stock of corn is treated as a wage fund. It is in this way that a convincing refutation can be produced against the criticisms made of the circulators of the annual produce. It can be argued that it is not the merchants who drive prices higher through their operations in the market, but rather it is the landlords through the increase of rent charges to the tenant farmer who contribute to such rapid price rises. However, this apparent shifting of ground involves more than a substitution of one culpable economic agent for another: it displaces the argument from the sphere of circulation to that of production. The demonstration of Malthus could be admitted, and with it much of the previous mode of considering the problem of agricultural prices; but it was possible to move the criticism to the landlord, with his monopoly position over the production of subsistence goods, able to increase at will the rents of his tenants and thus increasing the price of the goods to the population at large. By 1815, then, the problem of prices was no more the problem of marketing and distribution, but was concerned with the level of rents and the role of landlords in the economy.

It might be objected that this problem had been dealt with in the eighteenth century; but as shown in the previous chapter, Smith considered rent as a category worthy of attention because of the fact that it existed and had a real effect in the national economy. The treatment of rent was not related to any specific theorisation of economic relations, but rather his explanation of rent has recourse ultimately to the powers of nature and human desires (Smith, 1976, vol. II, p. 67)

As soon as the land of any country has all become private property, the landlords, like all other men, love to reap where they never sowed, and demand a rent even for its natural produce. The wood of the forest, the grass of the field, and all the natural fruits of the earth, which, when land was in common, cost the labourer only the trouble of gathering them, come, even to him, to have an additional price fixed upon them. He must then pay for the license to gather them; and must give up to the landlord a portion of what his labour either collects or produces. This portion, or, what comes to the same thing, the price of this portion, constitutes the rent of land, and in the price of the greater part of commodities makes a third component part.

Beginning from a statement to the effect that rent arises from payments for the use of property, Smith then relapses into 'human desires' to explain rent as an economic instance, and secondly attempts to argue that rent is simply a component of price. Buchanan, footnoting this passage editorially in 1814, questioned why the apparently unreasonable demands of the landlords should be so regularly complied with (Smith, 1814, vol. I, p. 80 fn. d). Smith had placed landlords as the agents who called rent into being by virtue of their control of land; rather, the problem was to explain rent as a distributive share without invoking such personal agency.

It was a Scottish farmer, James Anderson (1801, vol. V, p.403), who formulated the relation between price structure and rents when he argued that 'Rent is in fact nothing else than a simple and ingenious contrivance for equalising the profits to be drawn from fields of different degrees of fertility, and of local circumstances, which tend to augment or diminish the expense of culture.' This principle had been outlined earlier in 1777 in his *Observations on the Means of Exciting a Spirit of National Industry*; the 'profits' referred to here are of course what would be otherwise referred to as the 'gross return on capital advanced', but in general the relationship which Anderson proposes ensures a steady rate of profit on capital advanced under differing conditions of production. This conception of rent and price structure thus dispenses with the personal agency that Smith relied upon to account for the flow of rental payments from farmer to landlord, and appears to foreshadow the differential thesis that was to be characteristic of the rent theory of Classical Political Economy. But since the comment that Anderson made was by way of a comment on a system of circulation, and did not involve a consideration of the distribution of the product between the classes, it would not be justifiable to argue that this is an anticipation of

Classical rent theory. This theoretical centrepiece of Classical Political Economy did not simply arise as an abstraction from the existing forms of exchange in the economy, but was created by the forms of argument and theoretical work made possible in a new discursive form.

The most well-known statement of Classical rent theory is Ricardo's *Essay on the Influence of a Low Price of Corn on the Profits of Stock*, one of the pamphlets published in 1815. Certain revisions of the theory were made when he later published his *Principles*, but the general argument once sketched out has become recognised as the core of the Ricardian system. The 'Ricardian Rent Theory' relates the prices for agricultural products to the cost of production on the least productive land. This is a purely differential theory which relies on the fact that in agricultural production lands of different fertility and situation are combined together in the production of an annual crop. Commodities which sell for uniform prices in a national market are produced in situations which dictate varying costs of production. This was summarised by Ricardo (1951, vol. I, p. 67) in his *Principles* as follows:

> Rent is that portion of the produce of the earth, which is paid to the landlord for the use of the original and indestructible powers of the soil. It is often, however, confounded with the interest and profit of capital, and in popular language, the term is applied to whatever is annually paid by a farmer to his landlord. If, of two adjoining farms of the same extent, and of the same natural fertility, one had all the conveniences of farm buildings, and, besides, were properly drained and manured, and advantageously divided by hedges, fences and walls, while the other had none of these advantages, more remuneration would naturally be paid for the use of one, than for the use of the other, yet in both cases this remuneration would be called rent. But it is evident, that a portion only of the money annually to be paid for the improved farm, would be given for the original and indestructible powers of the soil; the other portion would be paid for the use of the capital which had been employed in ameliorating the quality of the land, and in erecting such buildings as were necessary to secure and preserve the produce.

The connection of 'rent' to the powers of the soil does not associate the theory of Ricardo with those of the eighteenth century that have already been considered; it is rather a means of discriminating between forms of capital, and as will be seen it does not interfere with the development of a theory of the distribution of the product which is independent of the conscious activity of the economic agents concerned.

Ricardo proposes that the extension of cultivation creates a rent which expresses the difference between two or more pieces of land.[4] An historical fiction is employed whereby all land is unimproved, and where initial cultivation of the most fertile land results in no rent being paid. In the 1815 *Essay* this is demonstrated by supposing that the capital employed on such land is of the value of 200 quarters of corn, half consisting of fixed, and half of circulating, capital. He then supposes that the fixed and circulating capital is replaced, and augmented by a return of 100 quarters, representing a profit of 50 per cent, without any deduction for rent. This rate of profit in turn regulates the rate of profit on capital employed in all other spheres. Under the pressure of population and the consequent necessity to produce more food, land of equal fertility, although less well situated, would be brought into cultivation; this would give rise to extra costs to produce the same gross product compared with that product obtainable on the first piece of land. If this extra cost were 10 quarters of corn, the capital laid out now will be 210 quarters, with a return of 100 quarters as before. The rate of profit on this capital consequently falls from 50 per cent to 43 per cent. (Ricardo, 1951, vol. IV, p. 13):

> On the land first cultivated, the return would be the same as before, namely, fifty per cent or one hundred quarters of wheat; but, the general profits of stock being regulated by the profits made on the least profitable employment of capital on agriculture, a division of the one hundred quarters would take place, forty-three per cent or eighty-six quarters would constitute the profit of stock, and seven per cent or fourteen quarters, would constitute rent. And that such a division must take place is evident, when we consider that the owner of the capital of the value of two hundred and ten quarters of wheat would obtain precisely the same profit, whether he cultivated the distant land, or paid the first settler fourteen quarters for rent.

As a result, profits of all stock fall to 43 per cent. The next step is to move with the same provisos of situation, or an alternative one of decreasing fertility, to the employment of 220 quarters, with the same return of 100 quarters, profits then falling from 43 per cent to 36 per cent (or 80 on 220), the rent of the first land correspondingly rising to 28 quarters, and commencing on the second portion of land at 14 quarters. This movement from better to worse soils is a pedagogic device intended to explicate the idea of differential returns in agricultural production and the relation of profit and capital to these returns. As rents rise, profits fall: what Ricardo did not develop explicitly was a conception of the price structure for agricultural commodities on which such movements are based. The principle of equalisation of returns to production that was so clearly stated by Anderson is only implied in the statement above. The 'Ricardian Rent Theory' is concerned principally with the mechanism for the generation and level of rent, rather than elaborating the conditions for its appropriation by a specific set of economic agents.

Consequently this 'Ricardian Rent Theory' is different from the 'Rent Theory' of Smith, no least because it is not justifiable to call Smith's comments on rent a theoretical statement. It represents, rather, some observations on the form an existent economic category takes, without seeking to integrate such observations into a coherent theory of distribution. The agrarian basis of Smith's conception of the economy is symbolised by his contention that it is the price of corn that regulates all other prices – and this conception was later rejected in the reorganisation of *The Wealth of Nations* by McCulloch in his 'Introductory Discourse' to the 1828 edition of Smith's work (1828, vol. I, p. lxx). Ricardo himself rejected this concentration on prices, and argued instead that the falling rate of profit is conditioned by agricultural production.[5]

Malthus's *Inquiry into the Nature and Progress of Rent, and the Principles by which it is Regulated* was published shortly before the essay by Ricardo, as were the other pamphlets by West and Torrens. He began by defining rent as follows (Malthus, 1970b, p. 179):

> The rent of land may be defined to be that portion of the value of the whole produce which remains to the owner of the land, after all the outgoings belonging to its cultivation, of whatever kind, have been paid, including the profits of the capital employed, estimated according to the usual and ordinary rate of the profits of agricultural stock at the time being.

Note that this does not, as in Smith, describe the rent paid as purely the produce of the soil, and the profits and wages as the produce of the labour input. Rent is simply seen here as a portion of the gross value produced, a residual which accrues to the landowner. The immediate occasion for the rent is described as the excess of price above the cost of production, but Malthus is careful to distance himself here from the Smithian conclusion that rent is therefore representative of monopoly powers. However, the mode in which he does this introduces some problems, since three causes of the 'high price' are distinguished (Malthus, 1907b, pp. 184–5):

(1) the special quality of land enabling a surplus to be produced over and above the maintenance of those who cultivate it;

(2) the quality that necessaries have of creating their own demand; and

(3) the comparative scarcity of the most fertile land.

(1) and (2) are then described as 'gifts of nature to man', assigning certain characteristics of agricultural production to the powers of nature in a fashion similar to the writers of the eighteenth century.

Whereas Ricardo (1951, vol. IV, p. 13 fn.) indirectly assumes that food commodities are distinct from all others, Malthus devotes the following two or three pages to a discussion of this proposition, and introducing 'demand' as the manner in which food goods are distinct; he suggests that in the case of food commodities the increase in demand is dependent on the production process itself, whereas in the case of all other commodities the demand is exterior to the process of production. Attention is then given to Sismondi's treatment of rent as solely the produce of labour, and Buchanan's argument that rent is simply a transfer payment (Malthus, 1970b, p. 190). These two positions are dismissed by the invocation of God and his relation to the powers of nature: 'Is it not, on the contrary, a clear indication of a most inestimable quality in the soil, which God has bestowed on man – the quality of being able to maintain more persons than are necessary to work it.' Having stated very clearly a 'naturalist' position, Malthus characteristically changes course once again and contrasts the earlier state of man, where usufruct rights prevailed, with the appropriation of the better soils by individuals and the rise of private property in land. Rent can then be reinstated as an economic category rather than as a natural one, and it becomes possible to formulate the price effects of rents and introduce a differential analysis of rent. In a fashion similar to Ricardo, the conception that rent is a payment for rights of use of specified portions of land is implied rather than being clearly stated; but while Ricardo appends a footnote in his *Essay* that states this, Malthus never does. Instead the narrative veers to the natural powers of the soil, describing the properties of the soil as 'a present to man of a great number of machines, all susceptible of continued improvement by the application of capital to them, but yet of very different original qualities and powers' (Malthus, 1970b, p. 207).

Whereas Smith was led at times to make the produce the source of rent, Malthus identifies differential fertility as the source. The consequence of this is to undermine the economic effectiveness of the distribution theory that Malthus develops; he argues that rent, as a residual payment, accrues to the landlords as the outcome of a natural gift to man, and is not primarily the payment for the use of land in a capitalist production process, varying inversely with profit and therefore the sign of an antagonism between landlord and capitalist. In the second edition of his *Principles of Political Economy* Malthus (1836, pp. 194–5) criticised the Ricardian position on rent as follows:

> If this view of the theory of rent were just, and it were really true, that the income of the landlord is increased by increasing the difficulty, and diminished by increasing the facility of production, the opinion would unquestionably be well founded. But if, on the contrary, the landlord's income is practically found to depend chiefly upon natural fertility of soil, improvements in agriculture, and inventions to save labour, we may still think, with Adam Smith, that the landlord's interest is not opposed to that of the country.

Thus the naturalist argument is deployed discursively by Malthus to establish harmony between landlord and capitalist, and as we shall see later this is then used to argue that in some ways the landlords are one of the most crucial classes in the economy. The theory of distribution that Malthus proposes arrives at different conclusions to those of Ricardo by virtue of this resort to Nature.

West took a different point of departure in his essay on rent to that of Ricardo and Malthus. He suggested that the principal problem was the diminishing returns that characterised agricultural production (West, 1815, p. 3):

> It is a fact acknowledged by all writers on political economy, that in the progress of improvement of any country, the productive powers of labour in agriculture improve less rapidly than the productive powers of labour in manufactures; or rather to express the same proposition more accurately, the productive powers of labour in raising rude produce improve less rapidly than the effective powers of labour in manufacturing it.

Developed from Smith's argument that the division of labour increases the productive powers of labour (the form in which capital and capital accumulation is thought of in *The Wealth of Nations*), West argues that the possibility of this in agricultural production is limited, since each unit of work added yields a diminished return so long as the quantity of labour input is not augmented continually. Considering first the effect of this on profits, West then introduces the problem of the price of corn and the level of rent and treats the already established labour differential as the principal element, rather than the fertility differential. The result is therefore a definition of rent which differs from that of Malthus: 'It is the diminishing rate of return upon additional portions of capital bestowed upon land that regulates, and almost solely causes, rent' (West, 1815, pp. 49–50). Because West deals with labour rather than fertility as the central element, there is no place in his analysis in which the 'natural powers' of Malthus can enter. For West, it is the productivity of labour that is significant, not of Nature. But on the other hand, West does not propose that rent is a payment for the use of land; rather, it arises because of the technical limitations of the division of labour in agricultural production. While the naturalist arguments of Malthus with respect to distribution are thereby avoided, which as we have seen result in rents falling to the landowner on account of the powers of Nature, West's argument places rents at the feet of the landowner because of the problem of the differential productivity of labour in agriculture.

In his *Essay on the External Corn Trade*, Torrens begins from the question of the high price of corn and its relation to the distribution of the crop through the year between harvests. In so doing he recapitulates the arguments advanced by Malthus in 1800 (Torrens, 1815, p. 8):

> By supplying the people, as nearly as they can judge, in this proportion, they [corn-dealers] are likely to sell their corn at the highest price, and with the greatest profit; and their knowledge of the state of the crop, and of the daily, weekly, and monthly sales, enables them to judge, with more or less accuracy, how far the markets are really supplied in this manner. Without intending to promote the interest of the public, corn dealers are necessarily led, by a regard to their own interest, to act in the manner most beneficial to the great body of consumers.

The development of stocks of corn in the hands of the dealers is a virtue, stabilising the market and enabling the farmer to receive a certain price for his product. In turn the farmer is better able to calculate the rent that he can afford to pay, and the level of investment that he can maintain in his farm. This argument is then linked to a comparison of the internal and external trades in corn, concluding that freedom in the foreign trade is of great advantage in stabilising seasonal irregularity and ensuring the most effective employment of capital at home (Torrens, 1815, pp. 44–5).

Strictly speaking Torrens does not develop a theory of rent, but rather one of profit, and this is done by considering the equalisation of the rate of profit between the manufacturing and agricultural sectors. A country is postulated where the prevailing rate of profit is 15 per cent in manufacture – and since there cannot be two rates of profit prevailing, it is only land which can return 15 per cent or more that will be cultivated. This will be so even if the resultant agricultural commodities are insufficient to sustain the population, for labour and capital will be most profitably employed in manufacture and any corn required will be imported. With the accumulation of capital in manufacture, however, the profit rate falls; it then becomes profitable to take in more agricultural land for cultivation, and so the process continues (1815, pp. 49–53). For Torrens, therefore, the question of distribution is one which concerns distribution between sectors of an economy, and not between classes. This is in turn related to the problem of ensuring a sufficient supply of corn – as is apparent, the rate of profit is conceived as a mechanism for distributing capital and labour between agriculture and manufactures, and the related movement of rents and wages as distributive shares is not considered. For Malthus and Ricardo, the economy has three classes which enter into the distribution of the product: landlord, capitalist, and labourer. For Torrens, on the other hand, the economy has two sectors for the purposes of distribution: manufacture and agriculture.

Ricardo developed a theory of rent which placed in a reciprocal relation rents and profits: with the accumulation of capital, the rate of profit would tend to decline, and as this occurred rents would rise steadily. Landlords, then, benefit from the accumulation of capital, while capitalist farmers, so long as they are able to compensate for the decline in the rate of profit by increased production, are indifferent. However, this conception of the process of distribution in capitalist production does set in play a joint antagonism between capitalists and landlords, an antagonism which is expressed in the *Essay* (1951, vol. IV, p. 21):

> It follows then, that the interest of the landlord is always opposed to the interest of every other class in the community. His situation is never so prosperous, as when food is scarce and dear: whereas, all other persons are greatly benefited by procuring food cheap. High rent and low profits, for they invariably accompany each other, ought never to be the subject of complaint, if they are the effect of the natural course of things.

The 'natural course' which is referred to here is quite distinct from the use which Malthus makes of naturalism, for it is here used to denote a specified mode of functioning of a commodity economy, dependent on the elaboration of an economic theory and not on the existence of God.

The theory of distribution that Ricardo formulates in his 1815 *Essay* expresses the joint antagonism of landlord and capitalist: between landlord and capitalist farmer within the sphere of agricultural production; and between landlord and manufacturing capitalist, i.e. between two spheres of production. The expression of the first antagonism is the debated category of ground-rent. The expression of the second is to be discovered in the debates on the price of food, and in the manner in which for the purpose of the clash of a nascent industrial capitalism with the landed interest and its protectionist policies the capitalist farmer found himself included in the 'landed interest'. This second level of the antagonism could be read as a continuation of the debates between agriculture and manufacturing sectors characteristic of Political Oeconomy. But what is at issue here is not an undifferentiated sector of a given polity, but rather the classes which constitute such sectors. And it is in this that we find registered one of the crucial indices of an economic discourse: instead of the untheorised conception of populations among whom a national product circulates, Classical Political Economy constructs distribution as occurring between theoretically defined economic agents. For the first time it is possible to construct economic, rather than political, legal or even human agencies which are derivative of a systematic analysis of production and distribution. The constitution of such specifically economic agencies, occupying a terrain of an economy, and not, as is the case with Political Oeconomy, a polity, is related to the possibility of constructing particular concepts of profit, capital, labour, value, and so on. This enables Ricardo to deduce specific economic 'interests' for each class, interests which are not derivative of the reality of landlords, farmers, or wage labourers *qua* persons, but which rather are strictly defined by the relations of profits, rents, wages, capital and accumulation of capital.

This is not to say that Ricardo's *Essay on Profits* states once and for all the central propositions of Classical Political Economy, or that this discursive form is a unity which expresses *tout court* economic discourse. While it can be said that Classical Political Economy is the first form in which an economic discourse is expressed, there are within it a number of unevenesses which are related to the way in which it utilises texts like *The Wealth of Nations* to express its central problems and constitute its mode of argument. It has already been noted how Malthus employs certain forms of argument which are associated with an eighteenth-century naturalism, with major consequences for the manner in which he defines the major object of political economy and conceives its proper area of investigation, as will be shown below. Ricardo, too, utilises certain untheorised formulations from Political

Oeconomy, most notably perhaps the conceptions of 'population' and 'subsistence'.

The Malthusian population doctrine (which is really a summary of the eighteenth-century argument on population) is concerned with the mode in which the population of a country regulates itself so that the numbers of inhabitants of a country are proportional to the means of subsistence. The problem identified by Malthus (1970a, p. 71), for which he has become renowned, was stated as follows:

> the power of population is indefinitely greater than the power in
> the earth to produce subsistence for men. Population, when
> unchecked, increases in a geometrical ratio. Subsistence increases only
> in an arithmetical ratio. A slight acquaintance with numbers will
> show the immensity of the first power in comparison of the second.
> By that law of our nature which makes food necessary to the life of
> man, the effects of these two unequal powers must be kept equal. This
> implies a strong and constantly operating check on population from
> the difficulty of subsistence. This difficulty must fall somewhere and
> must necessarily be severely felt by a large portion of mankind.

The numerical element of Malthus's reasoning is purely speculative, although he attempts to cite cases where population can be said to have increased at the rate that he suggests (1970a, pp. 73–5); the simultaneous development of the powers of agricultural production are on the other hand subjected to no such argument, and it is simply asserted that the geometrical growth of production is 'impossible to suppose' (1970a, p. 74). But it is sufficient to assume simply that there is the possibility of the rate of growth of population outstripping the rate of growth of production without assigning a specifically numerical quantity to this relation. Given this assumption, the problem then becomes one of accounting for the factors which consistently prevent the realisation of this tendency in persistent famine.

These factors were described as 'checks' by Malthus, and while there is some variation in the way that these were defined, they were resolved in his *Second Essay* of 1803 into the categories of vice, misery and moral restraint.[6] 'Misery' of course contains starvation, disease and premature death, and is the principal check on the growth of the poor – so the natural tendency for the labouring classes to increase is blocked by their inability to command the subsistence necessary for their support. This population principle is thus linked to a wage-fund theory which supposes that the sum of wages available is fixed, and the more wage-earners there are, the less each worker receives. As we will see, this is a perfectly reasonable supposition in an agrarian commodity economy, for the wage fund is resolvable into an annually harvested national product, a product which is fixed from year to year and which has to be distributed over time and within a population.

Ricardo's *Essay*, by expressing this commodity economy in terms of exchanges of corn, associated a wage fund directly with the allocation of means of subsistence. It can then be assumed that labourers receive a bare subsistence, and the question of wages is thereby neutralised through the invocation of Malthus's theory of population. These labourers are further dissolved into a 'population' which is endowed with an interest in low prices as opposed to the interest of the landlord. The twin usages of 'population' − to explain the receipt of subsistence wages by the labourer, and to express the unity of agents in an economy − are employed to focus attention on the antagonism between the landlord and the capitalist while neutralising other classes and economic relations. The condition for this being effective is that agricultural commodities are conceived as the only commodities of major importance; as we shall see in the next chapter, if this condition is not met, serious problems arise for the coherence of Classical Political Economy.

The antagonism between landlord and capitalist, which is central to the Ricardian theory of distribution, is condensed in the analysis of the generation and appropriation of ground-rent. Here both agents appear as equals: the landlord in possession of land as a means of production, and the capitalist in possession of the money necessary to hire this land and employ it in a capitalist production process. The analysis of distribution does not concern itself with the origin of the possessions of these agents: it is as irrelevant to consider the source of the capital held by the capitalist as it is to question the title of the landowner to his land. While a theory of distribution can account for the reproduction of these possessions in the hands of particular agents, it cannot and need not examine their mode of acquisition − for this falls outside the bounds of an economy. In this way the form of posing the relation between landowner and capitalist (or, more precisely here, tenant) in Political Oeconomy, where a landowner mysteriously extorts a revenue in the process of circulation from a 'defenceless capitalist', is decisively abandoned.

Malthus does not share this position. For him, rent is a quasi-natural phenomenon, and, as has been emphasised above, the 1815 *Essay* never clearly related ground-rent to rights of property. Instead, rent is 'natural', 'God-given', a residual share arising from differential fertility which falls into the laps of the landlords. Profits are not placed in a determinate relation with rents, as in Ricardo, but are rather independently located as residual incomes in a national economy. A consequence of this is that, unlike in Ricardo, landlords are not given any specific function in the distribution of the product, and it is possible to dismiss landowners as parasites in a fashion similar to Smith, their revenues derivative not of a distributive mechanism but of the powers of Nature. In short, landlords are inadequately constituted as economic agents by Malthus, and their presence in the economy can be construed as a contribution to disharmony.

This problem is rectified discursively by the deployment of a notion of 'effective demand' and its related categories, and the development of a theory of underconsumption as characteristic of the state of the economy. This theory of underconsumption in Malthus provides a substitute for the theory of distribution which Ricardo develops. However, Malthus's writings can be located firmly within the discursive formation of Classical Political Economy by virtue of the mode of analysis of landlord and capitalist, although the economic necessity of the landlords is retained by arguing that they consume the surplus that would otherwise lead to destabilisation and crisis. This transforms landlords from parasites to guarantors of the economy, and the conception of unproductive consumption is proclaimed as the necessary function of these economic agents.

Ricardo returned to the relation of landlords to the economy in his 1822 pamphlet *On Protection to Agriculture*, in which the argument against protection was continued, maintaining that it stagnated the economy by encouraging 'uneconomic' marginal production. The result was a tendency for the landlord's rent to be at a continuing high level, although the fluctuations faced by the farmer often meant that this high rent could not be paid (1951, vol. IV, pp. 238–9):

> It appears, then, that a high but steady price of corn is most
> advantageous to the landlord; but, as steadiness in a country situated
> as ours, is nearly incompatible with a price high in this country, as
> compared with other countries, a more moderate price is really for his
> interest. Nothing can be more clearly established, than that low prices
> of corn are for the interest of the farmer, and of every other class of
> society; high prices are incompatible with low wages, and high wages
> cannot exist with high profits.

The landed classes, by their control of the political apparatus, were able to maintain prices at a high level through the imposition of protectionist trade policies. Ricardo argued against such policies by stating that this disturbed the natural course of accumulation and general functioning of the economy – but the introduction of free-trade policies would not in fact alter the ecomonic relations which he had delineated. He suggested that free trade was in the interest of landed classes as well, since it was a means for the stabilisation of rents at an appropriate level for the farmers who had to pay them. This would therefore ensure adequate rents for the landlords, guaranteed profits for the farmer, and moderate prices for the population. Such legislative recommendations are not derived from the eighteenth-century 'strength of a nation' arguments but follow from an analysis of economic relations between agents constituted within a theory of distribution.

Shortly after the publication of his *Essay on Profits*, Ricardo was urged by James Mill to expand the argument and rewrite it, and with reluctance Ricardo began the necessary work. However, by October 1815 the project was already being treated by Mill as one aimed at the publication of a book. In November of the same year Mill was urging Ricardo to start at once on the subject of rent 'without an hours delay' (Sraffa, 1951, p. xiv). Drafting of a manuscript went ahead, although in the earlier part of 1816 Ricardo was increasingly pre-occupied with the difficulties of the concepts of 'value' and 'price'. Finally, by November 1816, the bulk of the manuscript was ready, and with some revisions the printing of it began in February 1817. On 19 April 1817 *On the Principles of Political Economy, and Taxation* was published, the text which was to become the principal expression of Classical Political Economy. The principal theoretical departure from the earlier *Essay* was the introduction of the problem of value in the first chapter, and the abandoning of the corn-economy analysis of the process of distribution.

We have already seen how the problem of value was circumvented by Ricardo in the 1815 *Essay* by his use of corn as representative of the commodity produced and of the commodities contributing to that production. Sraffa (1951, p. xxxi), in his introduction to Ricardo's *Principles*, outlines the form that this takes:

> The rational foundation of the principle of the determining role of the profits of agriculture, which is never explicitly stated by Ricardo, is that in agriculture the same commodity, namely corn, forms both the capital (conceived as composed of the subsistence necessary for workers) and the product; so that the determination of profit by the difference between total product and capital advanced, and also the

determination of the ratio of this profit to the capital, is done directly between quantities of corn without any question of valuation. It is obvious that only one trade can be in the special position of not employing the products of other trades while all the others must employ *its* product as capital. It follows that if there is to be a uniform rate of profit in all trades it is the exchangeable values of the products of *other* trades relatively to their own capitals (i.e. relatively to corn) that must be adjusted so as to yield the same rate of profit as has been established in the growing of corn; since in the latter no value changes can alter the ratio of product to capital, both consisting of the same commodity.

The virtue of this approach is that it enables the wage fund to be represented as a fixed stock of corn, and thus the problem of wages is dispensed with, following the demonstration by Malthus that the prices of corn were simply means for the apportionment of a 'corn fund' throughout the year. While it can then be shown (modifying this assumption) that wages and profits vary inversely, the major issue becomes the relation between rents and profits. The corn model makes possible the analysis of this relation without being side-tracked by problems of price and value, and without it being necessary to reduce the commodities involved to a common standard (Sraffa, 1951, p. xxxii). Another significant virtue of the corn model, which is hinted at above, is that it imposes a quite specific time on the processes of production and circulation of the produced good – corn is a commodity with a production period of one year, which requires for its production land (rent) and labour (wages); it then circulates for precisely one year while the next period of production elapses, the price of the good effecting this and being expressed in the level of rent. The specific temporal rhythm of production and circulation, combined with an assumption that sites of production differ in space and quality, render profit and rent specifically determined quantities, and enable the rate of profit in agriculture to determine the rate in all other trades.

The *Principles* replaces 'corn' with 'labour' and introduces the problem of value; but it should not be thought that by virtue of this the determining role of agricultural production is displaced. While the rate of profits is now determined by the ratio of the total labour of the country to the labour required to produce the necessaries for that labour, agricultural production is assigned a determining role in the process of capital accumulation, as will be seen below. At a more general level, the analysis of an economy is conceived as an analysis of capitalist agricultural production, and the first page of the *Principles* states this extremely forcefully (Ricardo, 1951, vol. I, p. 5):[7]

> The produce of the earth – all that is derived from its surface by the united application of labour, machinery, and capital, is divided among three classes of the community; namely, the proprietor of the land, the owner of the stock or capital necessary for its cultivation, and the labourers by whose labour it is cultivated.
>
> But in different stages of society, the proportions of the whole produce of the earth which will be allotted to each of these classes, under the names of rent, profit, and wages, will be essentially different; depending mainly on the actual fertility of the soil, on the accumulation of capital and population, and on the skill, ingenuity, and instruments employed in agriculture.
>
> To determine the laws which regulate this distribution, is the principal problem in Political Economy: much as the science has been improved by the writings of Turgot, Stuart, Smith, Say, Sismondi, and others, they afford very little satisfactory information respecting the natural course of rent, profit, and wages.

For Ricardo, political economy is the investigation of the system of distribution in an agrarian capitalist economy, in which the incidence of manufacture is subordinate. The corn model of 1815 had not then been a simple device to exclude the problem of value, an exclusion revoked in 1817; rather, it is in a more general sense representative of the form of organisation of the Ricardian system. As we shall see in the next chapter, once the homogeneity of agricultural commodity production is abandoned in favour of heterogeneous commodity production, the whole system of Classical Political Economy loses coherence and appears to be flawed. The attempt to rationalise the problem of value, and the search for an invariant measure of value, is an attempt to effect a generalisation of the classical system to heterogeneous commodity production. The category of value cannot in this way represent an 'essence' to Classical Political Economy, the achievement of an invariant measure enabling the theories of production and distribution to be applicable universally. It is the structure of these theories themselves which determines the form in which value as a category appears, and this category on its own does not possess the magical transformative powers to which it aspires.[8]

As was shown in Chapter 5, Smith conceived the accumulation of capital via his conception of the division of labour, linking forms of labour and the rate of accumulation. Ricardo completely alters this mode of connecting capital and labour, and in doing so inscribes land in a crucial and strategic position. In the chapters 'On Profits' and 'Effects of Accumulation on Profit and Interest', the following chain of events is proposed as consequent on increased investment in agricultural production: stimulation to population, with the resultant need to produce more food; extension of cultivation (or intensification), leading to a rise in costs of production and a rise in rents; a rise in amount paid out in wages; consequent decline in profits and eventual halt in the process of accumulation. The process of accumulation is then associated with the problem of augmenting the production of food which will subsist the labour employed by that capital accumulated. This is not, however, generalised into a theory of crisis, for factors such as foreign trade are invoked as tending to offset the arrival at a 'stationary state'. Ricardo employs Say's formulation that productions are bought with productions, i.e. that a generalised overproduction is not possible — no formal limit can therefore be set to the amount of accumulation possible in any country (Ricardo, 1951, vol. I, p. 290). The purpose of the schema outlined above is to emphasise that if wages are high, profits must necessarily fall; and this is shown by conceiving wages as a simple subsistence. The production of food, with the costs incurred and prices resulting, is given a crucial place in the argument of the relation between rate of profit and accumulation. Ricardo (1951, vol. I, p. 289) states it thus:

> If the funds for the maintenance of labour were doubled, trebled, or quadrupled, there would not long be any difficulty in procuring the requisite number of hands, to be employed by those funds; but owing to the increased difficulty of making constant additions to the food of the country, funds of the same value would probably not maintain the same quantity of labour. If the necessaries of the workman could be constantly increased with the same facility, there could be no permanent alteration in the rate of profits or wages, to whatever amount of capital might be accumulated.

The fact that the 'necessaries of the workman' cannot be increased with the same facility, as argued earlier (Ricardo, 1951, vol. I, p. 120), leads Ricardo to conclude that specific counteracting factors exist which prevent the realisation of the tendency of rate of profit to fall, and with it the disappearance of the incentive to invest or to switch capitals. This argument is used by Ricardo to criticise Smith's proposition that it is the scale of accumulation itself, with its concomitant increase in wages, that reduces the rate of profit. In particular, he suggests that Smith ignores the problem of subsisting the increased number of labourers employed by the additional capital (Ricardo, 1951, vol. I, p. 289).

Like much of the *Principles*, then, this process of formulation of a problem takes the form of a critique of *The Wealth of Nations*, either in asserting that Smith had not dealt adequately with a problem (for instance, the theory of rent), or in arguing that Smith's treatment is erroneous (as in the discussion of value). More generally, the structure of the *Principles* indicates that it was thought out with respect to a systematic and chapter-by-chapter critique of *The Wealth of Nations*. It has been argued that the apparently random order in which the topics appear in the *Principles* was a result of the somewhat haphazard way Mill dragooned Ricardo into writing. However, Sraffa (1951, p. xxiii) has shown that apart from the insertion of the discussion of rent as the second chapter, the order of the *Principles* follows closely that of *The Wealth of Nations*. This suggests that Ricardo wrote his text by working over the writing of Smith and constructing his own chapters and their order accordingly.

But there is one striking deviation to which Sraffa does not draw attention. The concordance of chapters of political economy places Ricardo's chapter 1 next to Smith's chapter 5; he simply ignores Book I, chs 1–4. An augmented concordance therefore appears overleaf (after Sraffa, 1951, p. xxiv).[9]

Ricardo does not simply re-order the topics that Smith deals with and produce a critique; by skipping the first sections of Book I of *The Wealth of Nations* Ricardo rejects vital elements of Smith's arguments. It was in these first four chapters that the relation of the division of labour to capital accumulation was established, and in particular the relation between productive and unproductive labour. As has been shown above, Ricardo criticised the manner in which Smith theorised capital accumulation, but more importantly the concept of labour in the *Principles* plays a quite novel role. For Smith, the term 'labour' is a device which enables him to account for the equalisation of exchanges, for the form of capital accumulation and for the general level of wealth of a nation. This last is effected by the division of the category 'labour' into productive and unproductive elements, so that the indiscriminate assessment of human activity that was possible in Political Oeconomy is blocked. For Ricardo, on the other hand, 'labour' is simply a commodity that can be used to express diverse and heterogeneous transactions, and which does not need to be called upon to perform any other theoretical work. In fact, the terms 'productive' and 'unproductive' labour, so

Smith, Book I	Ricardo
1 Of the Division of Labour	
2 Of the Principle which gives occasion to the Division of Labour	
3 That the Division of Labour is limited by the Extent of the Market	
4 Of the Origin and Use of Money	
5 Of the real and nominal Price of Commodities, or of their Price in Labour, and their Price in Money	1 On Value
6 Of the component Parts of the Price of Commodities	
	2 On Rent
	3 On the Rent of Mines
7 Of the natural and market Price of Commodities	4 On Natural and Market Price
8 Of the Wages of Labour	5 On Wages
9 Of the Profits of Stock	6 On Profits
10 Of Wages and Profit in the Different Employments of Labour and Stock	7 On Foreign Trade
11 Of the Rent of Land	

crucial to the analysis of *The Wealth of Nations*, are referred to only once in passing in the *Principles* – and this is when Ricardo quotes from Smith.

The passage in question is of interest, for it occurs in the chapter 'On Rent', where Ricardo (1951, vol. I, p 75) is criticising the notion that land is in some way privileged as an economic object by virtue of its relation to nature. A footnote is then appended in which a long quotation is taken from *The Wealth of Nations* where Nature is argued to produce rent (see above, p. 105). Ricardo notes that the powers of wind and water 'assist' in manufacture and trade, and then includes a quote from Buchanan which also argues that rent cannot be accounted for as a gift of Nature but must be related to the price mechanism (Ricardo, 1951, vol. I, p. 77 fn.). In the first quotation Smith mentions productive labour, and Buchanan refers to his own observations of productive and unproductive labour. It is in this context that the only comments on productive and unproductive labour to be found in Ricardo's *Principles* arise. The distinction of productive labour in Smith is related to the way in which Political Oeconomy takes a given polity and then has to identify the sectors or forms of activity that are 'economic'. On the other hand, Ricardo is concerned with the construction of theories of production and distribution on an economic terrain, within a discursive form that does not require a prior specification of appropriate sectors before analysis can begin. The categories of productive and unproductive labour are vital for Smith; they are irrelevant for Ricardo, since he is concerned with the production and distribution of commodities which are themselves defined by this process.

During 1816 it was the problem of value that had held up Ricardo's drafting of his book, and the question of the measure of value and its relation to price was to be one of the most commonly debated issues in the writings of Classical Political Economy. Such definitions and redefinition of 'value' practically without exception took their point of departure from the formulations of Smith. Unfortunately this was not without its problems, since Smith had proposed two distinct versions of value, one based on subjective estimation, and one based on labour-time embodied. Ricardo solved this dilemma by simply dismissing the first of these, a move consistent with the mode in which his arguments are formulated. But in the process of development which Ricardo instituted, two things occurred: first, the concept of value became derivative of a matrix of commodities, such that if the value of one commodity changed, the composition of the matrix altered; and second, progressively more attention was paid to the search for an invariant measure of labour.

The problematic search for a solitary and satisfactory measure of value is characteristic of the writings of the early nineteenth century, and Malthus (1820, p. 60) expressed the problem as follows:

> That a correct measure of real value in exchange would be very desirable cannot be doubted, as it would at once enable us to form a just estimate and comparison of wages, incomes, and commodities, in all countries and at all periods; but when we consider what a measure of real value in exchange implies, we shall feel doubtful whether any one commodity exists, or can easily be supposed to exist, with such properties, as would qualify it to become a standard measure of this kind. Whatever article, or even mass of articles, we refer to, must itself

be subject to change; and all that we can hope for is an approximation to the measure which is the object of our search.

The dilemma outlined by Malthus occupied other classical theorists, for they sought to extract elements from *The Wealth of Nations* and systematically reorganise them. In *The Wealth of Nations*, value (in both versions) is construed with respect to a collectivity of rationalising subjects, the population of a polity ruled by an invisible hand. The categories of the text are ordered according to this project; and this project is not one that is appropriate to Classical Political Economy.

However, the realist and naturalist aspects of Political Oeconomy can be traced in the way Malthus, for example, constructs his arguments. It has already been shown how this marks his analysis of rent; and it is clear that similar problems arise in his treatment of value. The notion of a *measure* of value is often thought with reference to an *origin* of value; and up until the early 1820s the variability of labour as a measure led Malthus (1820, pp. 127–9) to average it with corn, producing a corn/ labour standard on the basis of the dubious reasoning that in real conditions these two commodities varied inversely.

Ricardo (1951, vol. I, p. 29), in his departure from the work of Smith, was not concerned with value as the means of equalising exchange between differentiated individuals, but rather sought to utilise the term to investigate the relation between wages, profits and rents, and their distribution to landlords, capitalists and labourers. In doing this he abandoned the 'subjective' variant of Smith's value theory, and attempted to develop the notion of labour embodied as measure. This can be shown in his comments on Malthus's *Principles of Political Economy* (Ricardo, 1951, vol. II, pp. 24–5)

> In all that Mr. M. has yet said about exchangeable value, it appears to depend a great deal on the wants of mankind, and the relative estimation in which they hold commodities. This would be true if men from various countries were to meet in a fair, with a variety of productions, and each with a separate commodity, undisturbed by the competition of any other seller. Commodities, under such circumstances, would be bought and sold according to the relative wants of those attending the fair – but when the wants of society are well known, when there are hundreds of competitors who are willing to satisfy those wants, on the condition only that they shall have the known and usual profits, there can be no such rule for regulating the value of commodities.

The problem of the regulation of value coincides with the more abstract problem of the measure of value: for if there is a unique and unchanging measure of value, then this problem is disposed of.

When Malthus published his *Measure of Value Stated and Illustrated* in April 1823 he sought to represent his abandoning of the labour/corn measure of value (that had been outlined in his *Principles*) as a restatement of the Smithian orthodoxy that labour was the source of value. Ricardo responded to this by arguing that Malthus had thereby opted for 'a variable measure for an invariable standard' (Ricardo to Malthus, 29 April 1823; Ricardo, 1952, vol. IX, p. 282). In the correspondence which followed Ricardo sought to argue that the problem with Malthus's use of labour was that no account was taken of the conditions under which the quantity of labour bestowed was produced itself. These conditions could be various, and no statement of an 'invariable measure' was plausible unless it took account of these variations automatically. Further, there was also at issue the structural location of such a measure – money, for example, could be regarded as invariant in so far as its variation was only expressive of the value of a series of commodities which themselves fluctuated in value. Therefore, in a footnote at the beginning of the chapter on profits in the *Principles*, Ricardo (1951, vol. I, p. 110) remarks that 'for the purpose of making the subject more clear, I consider money to be invariable in value, and therefore every variation in price to be referable to an alteration in the value of the commodity'. But this very characteristic removed a consideration of money from theoretical investigation, and money pays a totally subordinate role in the structure of Classical Political Economy.

In August 1823, shortly before his death, Ricardo began drafting a paper which summarised his disagreements with Malthus, and these notes on 'Absolute and Exchangeable Value' serve to emphasise the divergence of Ricardo from the crude 'labour theory of value' that has often been attributed to him. Here Ricardo restated his argument that 'a day's pay' could not be the basis of an invariable measure since this quantity differed in various countries. However, this gesture to other countries was accompanied by postulated times of production with different compositions of capital and labour, in which the former could also be treated as advances necessary to subsist the labourer during the period of production. Rejecting both Malthus's version of Smith's theory, and also Smith's conception of 'estimation' and cost of production, Ricardo argued that it was possible to isolate an invariable measure of value, on the condition that a commodity was isolated along with its contributory commodities that were subject to variation. It was the matrix which these commodities formed that provided the necessary principle of invariability (Ricardo, 1951, vol. IV p. 364).

Ricardo was himself in turn accused of using a variable measure for an invariable standard by Bailey (1825, p. 4), who counterposed to the Ricardian 'deviation' the substantial rectitude of Smith's definition of value as the power of purchasing other goods. Bailey (1825, p. 5) mounted his criticism of all the Classical Economists on the grounds that value could not be the attribute of a commodity *per se*, but could only express the relation between two objects as exchangeable commodities: 'As we cannot speak of the distance of any object without implying some other object, between which and the former this relation exists, so we cannot speak of the value of a commodity but in reference to another commodity compared with it.' The form in which Malthus had been criticised by Ricardo was itself criticised by Bailey (1825, p. 17), who argued that labour could be invariable only with respect to those commodities which were directly related to it. But in making this criticism it can be suggested that Bailey is drawing on a realist conception of the commodity economy in which the theoretical arguments and terms have to be based on the conditions existing in a specific national economy. As we have seen, Ricardo was not free himself from such assumptions: in Bailey, however, they come to dominate the mode of criticism that he engages. The problem of 'value' in Classical Political Economy is a complex and often impenetrable one, and even Ricardo noted that it was a problem quite irrelevent to the treatment of the distribution of wages, profits and rent which he regards as the major concern of political economy (Ricardo to McCulloch, 13 June 1820; Ricardo, 1952, vol. VIII, p. 194).

'Circulation' is of concern to Classical Political Economy only in so far as it denotes the arena in which the price mechanism operates, and in the case of Ricardo can affect the allocation of capital via the category of population. The term has no effectiveness beyond this, and the discursive function performed in Political Oeconomy is erased in the structure of economic discourse. There are certain resonances, however, as when Ricardo (1951, vol. I, p. 31) distinguishes fixed from circulating capital according to the rate at which they enter circulation, recapitulating the eighteenth-century conception of 'perishability'. In the second and third editions of the *Principles* Ricardo sought to neutralise this statement by appending a footnote stating that the distinction was not essential, the demarcation not clear.[10] The association of capital with a process of circulation was, on the other hand, interdicted in Classical Political

Economy by the manner in which the concept was formulated. Unlike Political Oeconomy, which employed the term in a fashion that did not distinguish it absolutely from the personal wealth of the persons constituting the polity, for Classical Political Economy 'capital' is an economic category with a specific function which is distributed by means of the mechanics of capital flow. In the Ricardian corn economy, it is the advances of corn which are equated with capital, rendering the distinction of capital-forms unnecessary, and even in the *Principles* Ricardo's definition (1951, vol. I, p. 95) of capital as 'that part of the wealth of a country which is employed in production, and consists of food, clothing, tools, raw materials, machinery etc. necessary to give effect to labour' is not incompatible with such a conception. Capital is simply the means to further production, and conceived as such there can be no internal limitation to its accumulation.

If, however, capital is divided into fixed and circulating components, it is possible to argue that fixed capital consists primarily in machinery; and the accumulation of machinery-capital can under certain conditions be represented as an internally contradictory process. Such a representation was made by certain economists in the 1820s, formulating what came to be known as a 'theory of underconsumption'. This conception is of course distinct from the notion of 'gluts', a term which carries with it agricultural connotations and the implication that the surplus is a temporary phenomenon that can be corrected by a fall in the price of the product; 'underconsumption' here appears as a literal alimentary metaphor where the yearly consumption of the agrarian product must be effected at a suitable price to enable production to continue.

Malthus is of course the major exponent of this latter variation, deriving, as was suggested above, a theory of unproductive consumption on the part of landlords as a substitute for a satisfactory theory of distribution. The gluts that landlords prevent are either of a strictly agrarian form or are the outcome of a disproportionality between the agrarian and manufacturing sectors. The existence of the landlord class *qua* economic agent is related not to the manner in which it is constituted by an analysis of distribution, but rather to the exigencies of the laws of nature (Malthus, 1836, pp. 398–9):

In the fertility of the soil, in the powers of man to apply machinery as a substitute for labour, and in the motives to exertion under a system of private property, the laws of nature have provided for the leisure or personal services of a certain portion of society; and if this benificent offer be not accepted by an adequate number of individuals, not only will a positive good, which might have been so attained, be lost, but the rest of society, so far from being benefited by such self-denial, will be decidedly injured by it.

Malthus (1836, p. 375) tended in addition to this to invoke a 'middle class' of consumers to assist the landlords in their task of social disposal, boosting in this way the effective demand in the economy. Thus 'effective demand' is deployed as the complementary mechanism to the gains from Nature which result in the surplus in the sphere of production; it ensures the existence of an equilibrium between the spheres of production and consumption and the 'eating up' of the produced surplus. When Say (1821, p. 301) criticised Malthus in a series of letters, it was this use of the category 'demand' that was one of the main points of criticism:

> It is with the rent of land, the interest, and the salaries, which form the profits resulting from this production, that the producers purchase the articles of their consumption. Producers are at the same time consumers; and the nature of their wants, having an influence, in different degrees, on the demand for different productions, always favours, when liberty exists, the production of that which is most necessary, because, being the most in demand, it immediately becomes the article which yields the greatest profit to enterprisers.

Say reiterates that demand cannot be an appropriate problem for Classical Economics, for once it is introduced a rapid collapse into some form of underconsumptionism is the result. In an agrarian commodity economy, a glut can only be of a temporary nature, partly by virtue of the form of agricultural production, and partly because the principle of population is employed to adjust labour to product in the long run.[11]

The transfer of the agrarian theory of 'gluts' to industrial production in Classical Political Economy was effected by associating fixed capital with machinery. The traditional argument initiated by Ricardo in 1817 was that any labour displaced by the introduction of machinery would be automatically absorbed elsewhere (McCulloch, 1821, pp. 115–19). The increased productive power of machinery was a simple addition to capacity which was not conceived as having any serious consequences for the functioning of an economy. Since products were bought with products, there was no way in which unemployment could be conceived as a result of the widespread use of machinery – the increased production itself ensured that more employment was available.

Contemporary literature on the rise of factory production betrayed little concern with the possibilities of widening unemployment, and in fact the principal evil of the new factories was conceived as the moral harm done by mixing operatives of both sexes during the working hours. This being so, the few comments on the use of machinery that can be found prior to 1820 welcome its employment, since the greater regulation of the labour process that results minimises the opportunities for sexual license (Smart, 1910, p. 226).

Accordingly Ricardo had in the first two editions of the *Principles* argued that the use of machinery benefited labourer and capitalist alike. However, this benefit would only be registered in the profits of the capitalist, since the wage-fund/population theory ensured that a rise in wages would tend to increase the population and lower wages back to their original level. In 1817 John Barton wrote to Ricardo questioning this set of propositions, and Ricardo responded by simply reaffirming his original position (Ricardo to Barton, 20 May 1817; Ricardo, 1952, vol. VII p. 157). Later that year Barton published his *Observations on the Circumstances which Influence the Condition of the Labouring Classes of Society*, in the course of which some calculations were produced purporting to demonstrate that the progressive introduction of machinery had a tendency to create unemployment. This was followed with a series of alternative mixes of capital and labour as options under differing prevailing levels of wages and profits (Barton, 1817, pp. 15–19). The general argument of this text, though nowhere clearly spelled out, was that machinery, far from being a benign and non-disruptive influence on the economy, was destined to interrupt the hitherto ordered workings of the economy. The cost of this disruption was to be borne by the working class in the shape of a steadily increasing rate of unemployment. Ricardo responded to this argument by reconsidering his position on the effects of machinery. Thus in the third edition of the *Principles* he inserted a new chapter to correct what he now conceived to be his earlier error with respect to the employment of the labouring classes (Ricardo, 1951, vol. I, p. 388):

My mistake arose from the supposition, that whenever the net income of a society increased, its gross income would also increase; I now, however, see reason to be satisfied that the one fund, from which landlords and capitalists derive their revenue, may increase, while the other, that upon which the labouring class mainly depend, may diminish, and therefore it follows, if I am right, that the same cause which may increase the net revenue of the country, may at the same time render the population redundant, and deteriorate the condition of the labourer.

It can be seen here that the revision that Ricardo introduces is argued out with respect to the relations between the economic agents that have already been established theoretically, and his conclusion concerning the possible unemployment of labourers is not drawn from a reflection on the use of machinery in factories as such. Nevertheless, the modification that Ricardo felt he had to introduce when discussing the form of organisation of an industrial commodity economy met with a speedy reaction from McCulloch, who stated in a letter to Ricardo that the addition of the chapter on machinery seriously modified the argument of a text that he had regarded until then as the epitome of the new economics. He even here accused Ricardo of conceding the arguments, so recently rejected by Ricardo, that Malthus had proposed in his *Principles* concerning underconsumption, (McCulloch to Ricardo, 5 June 1821; Ricardo, 1952, vol. VIII, p. 382).

It is clear that the addition of a chapter on machinery to the *Principles* does not seriously alter the nature of the theories of production and distribution that are there advanced. These theories were derived from the analysis of commodity production and circulation in an agrarian economy, where rent plays a crucial role in regulating the disposition of the discursive elements. As Ricardo (1952, vol. VIII, p. 194) wrote to McCulloch in 1820, it was by 'getting rid of rent, which we may do on the corn produced with the last capital employed' that enabled capital and labour to be considered as directly related agencies. But this 'disposal' of the problem of rent is not a simple dismissal, for the category of rent in the Classical System is vital, since it is the distributive share whose variation controls the respective shares of capital and labour. The last two categories receive revenues which are posed in a directly inverse relation – as wages go up, profits go down. In fact, it would be more correct to argue that Ricardo 'gets rid of' wages, not rent, and that he does this by introducing the wage-fund/population principle. Wages can then be assumed to be stable, and the variation introduced by the increase or decrease of agricultural production, with the effects on rent and profits, can then be investigated.

Ricardo's remarks on machinery represent a reflection on the status of the simple association of the wage fund with the labour available for employment. In fact, the creation of unemployment can be accommodated by arguing that this 'excess labour' represents excess population, and all that happens is an automatic adjustment to the prevailing means of employment. But Ricardo sought to incorporate some of the features of industrial commodity production in his basically agrarian model, a model which quite adequately established the conditions of existence of economic agents as long as they were confined to agricultural commodity production. McCulloch was of course wrong to see in the considerations on machinery a convergence with Malthus; the economic agents that Ricardo had constituted were not affected by the introduction of such a disruptive factor. On the other hand, Malthus arrived at a theory of underconsumption precisely because the conditions of existence of landlords as economic agents remained unsecured in his theory of rent. As we shall see in the following chapter, it was only when the theory of rent was omitted from a theory of distribution that the Ricardian mode of constituting agents fell into disarray, a disarray which signalled the end of Classical Poltical Economy as a plausible analysis of the economy.

We have seen in chapter 3 how in the seventeenth century the economy is instituted by political agents, providing the function of exchanges between such agents and guaranteeing their subsistence, or reproduction, as agents. On the other hand, economic discourse makes possible the constitution of specifically economic agents, agents that are not related to 'real persons', rational calculators or whatever: they are constituted discursively by relations of capital and labour, categories which themselves are formulated discursively. The terms 'land' and 'labour' are in the discursive forms that we have been considering subject to a series of dislocations; and it has been part of the argument of this book that these terms cannot be anything other than the vehicles for a series of problems which in no way are inscribed as 'essential meanings' within the terms themselves. 'Land' and 'labour' are not terms whose comprehension involves a reference to a real economy for their import to be assessed: they are parts of divergent systems which themselves constitute discursively these 'real economies'. The crucial distinction of Classical Political Economy from Political Oeconomy is that it does not depend on the prior existence of a polity for it to identify an arena of investigation – this arena is constituted discursively by its theories of production and distribution. Classical Political Economy does not provide a universal solution to the problems that arise on this terrain, however, for it relies crucially on its theory of rent to effect its analysis of commodity production. If this theory of rent is set aside, then a series of difficulties arise that can only be resolved by a recasting of the original problems.

7
The Dissolution of Classical Political Economy

While Classical Political Economy is not reducible to the structure of an agrarian commodity economy realised in a specific time and space, it did provide the means for constructing arguments concerning the appropriate mode of regulation of this economy. Thus, as we have seen, formulations concerning the levels of profit and the distribution of the means of production in agriculture could be converted into supports for legislative positions. It would be quite erroneous, however, to conceive this remobilisation of theoretical statements into political argument as the casual *raison d'être* of these statements. As was argued in the previous chapter, it is possible to evaluate the texts produced by Malthus and Ricardo without resort to conceptions of 'ideology' or 'political interest', terms which by invoking conceptions of expressivity and class position of subject – author invoke immediately the 'real' as a privileged meta-discourse. Economic discourse is not a discursive form which has a its object 'the economy' as a prior and unconditioned entity; the validity of statements formed within economic discourse cannot be derived from this supposed object, with its epistemological ambiguities, but can only be assessed according to the rules of formation of economic statements. Changes in the form of organisation of an economy do not therefore provoke adjustments in the mode of organising economic statements – for economic theory is not an expression of an economy, and so cannot be transformed by any alterations the latter undergoes. What does happen is that the process of mobilising theoretical statements (formed in an economic discourse) into the supports of various political arguments undergoes a displacement. And this chapter will examine briefly the displacement that occurs with respect to Classical Political Economy as a specific discursive form.[1]

As I outlined in the previous chapter, Classical Political Economy constituted economic agents and modes of exchange between these agents with concepts of capital and profit that were related to the organisation of an agrarian commodity economy. Consequently, it was possible to utilise certain conclusions of this structure in the contemporary debates on the Corn Laws and agricultural protection, while at the same time Classical Political Economy was not reducible to these forms of argument. Rather, it was mobilised as a mode of proof of particular political positions.

By the later 1820s, however, the nature of the economy was changing, turning away from agriculture and becoming progressively marked by the rhythms of industrial commodity production. The registration of this is apparent in the way that the growth of an urban working class as a social problem suddenly appears in writings of this time. No longer is it the landlord who represents an economic problem, it is the worker, unskilled, illiterate and consigned to long hours of work in the new mills whose conditions formed the subject of a growing number of investigations. Furthermore, this new class threw up its own spokesmen, who, basing their analysis on the established works of the Classical Economists, argued that the wages received by the working class as its distributive share were only a part of what should by right be theirs – and that the profits of the capitalists only existed by virtue of the robbery of the workers. Responding to these arguments (and the strikes and riots which expressed them, in a different fashion), a series of economists began a revision of the established forms of economic argument, seeking to establish an analysis of distribution that could adequately account for the respective determination of wages and profits. The arguments and forms of explanation that this project necessarily involved could find no purchase in the Classical Theory of Distribution, determinate as it was only by virtue of the presence of rent. To consider simply wages and profits within the Classical Scheme rendered the constitution of economic agents that it involved incomplete; and it therefore appeared that errors had been located in Classical Political Economy, errors which rendered the whole system vulnerable. But as will be shown below, this evaluation is a result of generalising a theory of distribution which for a one-commodity, monotonic production period economy requires the existence of the category of rent to effect its constitution of economic agents.

Criticism of the Classical System can be found in the manner in which, at the end of the 1820s, Ricardo was no longer attacked as the betrayer of Smith, but rather simply as an anachronism. This can be seen at work in the minutes of the Political Economy Club, a dining club set up to provide a debating forum between prominent economists of the day. In January 1831, Torrens argued that all the major points of Ricardo's *Principles* had been abandoned, and that the theories of value, rent and profits found there were erroneous. Faced with the dismissal of all the salient principles of Ricardian economics, McCulloch's defence was, at the least, equivocal (Political Economy Club, 1921, p. 224):

> 'McCulloch stood up vigorously for Value as well as Rent, and paid very high compliments to Ricardo, whom he still considered as right in most points, and at all events as having done the greatest service to the science, his methodical and scientific way of treating it, so that even where he was mistaken, his errors could be detected by a subsequent and more correct analysis.

In a later meeting of the Club Ricardo was in some respects reinstated, but it is clear from the nature of economic debates in the 1830s that Ricardianism was dissolved as a coherent system of economic analysis. Instead a distinct body of theory was emerging, one that addressed itself to the problems of distribution, but utilising different means to construct the agents and forms of exchange between these constituted agents.

The work of Senior, Longfield, Torrens and Scrope among others is representative of these attempts to account for price formation and capital accumulation under conditions of heterogeneous commodity production, where the periods of production in various alternative investments altered crucially the measured swing of the agrarian cycle. These names have become recognised as belonging to the phase of 'vulgar apologetics' which followed the high phase of bourgeois scientific political economy, characterisations that were first made by Marx. Such judgments, condemning the work of certain economists on the grounds that their proposals involved a specific class position, are of the type that have been criticised repeatedly in the course of this book.[2] Marx argued that the theoretical statements of these writers failed to penetrate the surface of the capitalist economy, whose appearance concealed the real, inner laws of working that Marx himself claimed to have located. But to effect such an argument involves the kinds of epistemological evaluation of discourse that has been argued above to be inappropriate. It is not possible here to discuss the criticisms that Marx advanced against these so called 'vulgarians', besides noting that the mode of analysis it involves is in conflict with the one that is set to work here; and that, perhaps more decisively, the use of such forms of argument results in a simple dismissal of crucial problems in the formation of economic analysis.

The late 1820s saw two major responses to the crisis in Classical

Political Economy: the revision by the Ricardian socialists; and the rejection by the new school of economists. But there was another response to be found, although the essays were not published until 1844: John Stuart Mill's *Essays on some Unsettled Questions of Political Economy*. Although originally drafted in the years 1829–30, four out of the five remained in manuscript because, Mill (1844, p. v) wrote, of the 'temporary suspension of public interest in the species of discussion to which they belong'. The 'suspension' was not of course in economic debate *per se*, but rather in the Ricardian orthodoxy that Mill had been drilled in since his youth by his father, James Mill. Accordingly these essays attempt to modernise the Ricardian doctrine without abandoning the central bases of the theories of production and distribution that are specific to it.

The fourth essay in this collection is on profits, and it is here that Mill attempts to recover the orthodox Ricardian treatment of distribution. Unlike Ricardo's *Essay on Profits* of 1815, which relied on the conception of differential rent to construct the analysis of profits and capital accumulation, Mill here ignores rent altogether and considers in turn profit, wages and interest. Profit, it is argued, cannot be attributed to the productive power of capital, or of land (Mill, 1844, pp. 90–1):

The 'productive power of capital', though a common, and, for some purposes, a convenient expression, is a delusive one. Capital, strictly speaking, has no productive power. The only productive power is that of labour; assisted, no doubt, by tools, and acting upon materials. That portion of capital which consists of tools and materials, may be said, perhaps, without any great impropriety, to have a productive power, because they contribute, along with labour, to the accomplishment of production. But that portion of capital which consists of wages has no productive power of its own. Wages have no productive power; they are the price of a productive power. ... That portion of capital which is expended in the wages of labour, is only the means by which the capitalist procures to himself, in the way of purchase, the use of that labour in which the power of production really resides.

Those who were at this time beginning to discover in this power of 'capital' for producing profit and interest the justification of the appropriation of profit and interest by the capitalist are here opposed by Mill, who asserts that labour is the source of productiveness. But this argument is elaborated by Mill in a reversion to the distinction of productive and unproductive forms of labour, a distinction which, as

was shown in the previous chapter, had been rejected by Ricardo. In a
separate essay on the definition of these terms, Mill proceeds to
enumerate the different forms of labour and evaluate them by
distinguishing the mode of production of an object or service and its
mode of consumption. Underlying these distinctions is a combination of
a notion of exchange value inflected through a conception of utility
which is opposed to enjoyment. By manipulating these categories Mill
(1844, pp. 84–6) is able to allocate different professional categories into
productive or unproductive classes; and the possibility is thus opened up
of establishing the national economy as a collectivity whose population
can be simply constituted on this basis. The conceptions of consumption
and utility that Mill introduces to combat the idea that capital produces
value result in the appearance of the subjective categories of economic
action that were typical of the writings of Senior and Longfield.

The analysis of distribution that Mill proposes concerns two agents
only : capitalist and labourer. The capital of the capitalist is in this version
advances held by that agent on which a return must be made in order for
the process of production to continue. However, these advances are
accumulated labour, for 'Labour alone is the primary means of production;
"the original purchase-money which has been paid for everything".
Tools and materials, like other things, have originally cost nothing but
labour; and have a value in the market only because wages have been
paid for them' (Mill, 1844, p. 94). But, again, this assertion of the pre-
eminence of labour is unsupported by the Malthusian population
principle that Ricardo adopted, and also lacks the argument concerning
the subsistence of labour as its price. The opposition to contemporary
economists who considered capital as productive *sui generis* appears at
first to restore a Ricardian orthodoxy; but by omitting the crucial
category of rent from the order of constituting economic components,
Mill reduces the Ricardian system to disarray and results in a
convergence with the very theoreticians that Mill was attempting to
oppose. In Ricardo's *Essay on Profits*, the level of profits was determined
by the level of rent, and wages were assigned third place in this order,
permitted to fluctuate inversely with profits but retained within limits by
the untheorised principle of population. Mill undermines this, and by
omitting the category of rent removes the discursive conditions for the
effectiveness of this theory of profits and wages. All that is left is the
elementary principle that as wages go up, profits go down, and *vice
versa*, plus the tenet that labour is the source of wealth.

The Classical Theory of Distribution hinged on a dual relation
between landlord and capitalist as economic agents; Mill's attempt to

revise this and produce a theory based on the confrontation of capitalist and labourer founders on the fact that the Classical Theory relied on an untheorised set of principles to account for the existence and level of wages. A further consequence is that the capitalist cannot be adequately constructed as an economic agent, since his presence is only required as the advancer of that which originates with the labourer in the first place. The attempt to revise Classical Political Economy into a consistent theory of wages and capital thus collapses into the theories that Mill was attempting to refute.

Longfield, whose *Lectures* are representative of the tendency that Mill had attacked, is notable for his explicit attempt to construct an analysis of distribution which did not base itself on the discursive priority of rent or labour. Mill had abandoned the first and attempted to argue that the second category was central to economic analysis; but the neglect of rent while retaining the bases of Classical Political Economy leads to results not dissimilar to those outlined by Longfield. The 'Preface' to *Lectures on Political Economy* argues against the assumption in *The Wealth of Nations* that the annual product goes first to labour as wages, and that it is the remainder that is distributed as profits and rents. He proposes instead to invert this order, and show that rent and profits are prior to wages. This procedure will enable him to construct a theory of wages that does not consist in the simple inverse movement that Mill proposed, and furthermore it has the advantage of not assuming that the level of wages necessarily corresponds to the level of subsistence required by labour. 'Labour', the organising category of Mill's analysis, is disenfranchised and made conditional upon the movement of capital and profits.

Accompanying this denial of the constitutive role of labour is its corollary in the criticism of its use as the measure of value often asserted, on the grounds that it entered in some part into the production of most commodities. This quality of labour, Longfield (1834, p. 31) argued, could not be utilised to elevate labour into a unique measure of the value of commodities, since any commodity can serve as such a measure, providing 'its value admits of being compared directly with that of the article whose value is being measured'. Labour is just a commodity: thus it has no special privilege inscribed in it which endows it with universality as a measure of value, nor of being constitutive of value by virtue of this universality. The centrality of 'labour' in economic discourse marks the presence of a philosophical anthropology that can be localised or neutralised (as in Ricardo) but which retains its effectiveness by virtue of the 'workmanship' model of labour and property outlined in chapter 3. In its most vulgar form, this conception of property and action, whereby it is the action of a subject on an object which defines the terrain of the economy and constitutes economic objects, becomes congruent with economic discourse *per se*, reworking the variant forms of economic discourse into diverse configurations of this eternal presence of labour as the essential mode of being.

Longfield rejects the argument that labour constitutes economic objects, but he replaces this with the idea that economic objects are constituted by 'scarcity', thus reintroducing immediately the subjectivism that had just been dismissed. The presence of a benevolent Nature and a subject charged with particular desires and interests ensures that the process of constitution and circulation of objects is regulated (1834, p. 44):

> However useful, or even necessary to the subsistence of man, any commodity may be, there is a limit to the quantity of it which any individual can consume, and the love or necessity of variety will induce him to part with all that he possesses beyond a certain share, if by parting with it he can procure anything which can contribute more to his enjoyments. And by a wise provision of nature, the more indispensable any commodity is to human subsistence or happiness, the more strict and absolute is the limit within which our consumption of it is confined. The most natural and most urgent of our appetites are those which can be the soonest and most certainly satisfied. Those which in their extent are the most insatiable, can be repressed or denied without any diminution to our happiness. By this provision the riches of the wealthy are prevented from interfering with the maintenance of the poor.

It might appear that this formulation approximates to the one made by Lauderdale (1804, p.12), when he suggests that value is conferred first by the fact of a commodity being desirable to man, and second that it should exist in a state of scarcity. But the distinction that Longfield introduces is that the 'supply' of the 'scarce objects' is governed ultimately, not by a benevolent or miserly 'nature', but rather by the cost of production of these objects. The conception of scarcity is thus detached from a naturalisation of the economic order, and located as an object of economic investigation.

The assumption made by the Classical Economists was that labour received in wages the revenue necessary to subsist a given labour force, although, as we have seen, this was qualified by the conception of a wage fund of subsistence goods and the Malthusian population principle.

On the other hand, Longfield (1834, pp. 20–4) denies that there is any natural connection between the remuneration of labour and the cost of production of labour. This follows from the denial that the value of a commodity is governed by the labour employed in its fabrication – such that the labour embodied in the maintenance of labour itself cannot determine its value. Labour is simply a commodity which has a value determined by the operation of the forms of supply and demand, forms which (potentially at least) are subject to specific conditions of existence. Labour has no natural right to a specific sum of wages after which the profit of the capitalist and the rent of the landlord can be determined; it is paid out of the advances of capital. Such advances will only be forthcoming if the entrepreneur is ensured of a profit on the transaction, and thus is derivative of the existence of profit as a distributive share, not constitutive of it (1834, p. 170):

> ...the employer pays wages to the labourer according to a contract
> made between them. He pays the wages immediately, and in return
> receives the value of his labour, to be disposed of to the best
> advantage. The employer does this for the sake of the profit which he
> expects to make by the transaction. Hence the value of the labour
> fixed in, or transferred to, any article, is greater than the wages of that
> labour. The difference is the profit made by the capitalist for his
> advances: it is, as it were, the discount that the labourer pays for
> prompt payment.

Capital, then, is a stream of advances over time, and the rate of profit is a return on the time for which these advances remain unrecouped. There is no cost of production as such for capital, only a change of use of resources into such advances. Wages represent costs to be covered by advances which are no different in kind to other raw materials acquired in the process of organising the production of commodities. This process of production of commodities can be resolved into labour and time in which the remuneration of labour is dependent on the rate of profit that the capitalist is able to realise from the combination of the elements of production (Longfield 1834, pp. 215–16). The process of circulation is effected by a series of mediators who transmit the product from the execution of the labour to the consumer of the product, each mediator handling the product for a rate of profit proportional to the time of circulation of the advances made. The division of the revenue from the ultimate sale of such a product between capitalist and labourer will therefore depend on the time elapsed between time of execution and time of sale, the amount of profit rising proportionately the longer this period is (Longfield 1834, p. 211).

The analysis of value and production that Longfield presents was used by him to demonstrate that the demand that labour should receive a 'full remuneration' of the labour embodied was without rational foundation; combinations of workmen could not therefore raise wages, nor, for that matter, could capitalists. This of course involves a utilisation of the foregoing analysis for political ends, but it is important to stress the economic coherence of this argument. It is not justifiable to reduce such economic analysis to the bad faith of a reactionary who wishes to prove the impossibility of the demands of organised labour. The great merit of Longfield's analysis is that it breaks with the conditions of classical analysis and inaugurates in a systematic manner a new mode of dealing with profit and wages, and their relation to the formation of prices in a heterogeneous commodity economy. The introduction of time is crucial to this project, for once the regularity of the agrarian commodity economy is no longer constructed as a discursive condition, the processes of production and circulation become a major theoretical problem.

Other writers in the 1830s, such as Senior and Scrope, rejected the conceptions of production and distribution that informed Classical Political Economy, placing emphasis rather on the power of capital and the necessary remuneration of the capitalist for production to continue. Senior in his *Three Lectures on the Rate of Wages* states explicitly that his principal object was to demonstrate the falsity of the economic principles embodied in the demands of the working class, and to do so he effectively recapitulated the argument that Malthus had first advanced in 1800. In the case of Senior however, the wage fund was not conceived as a corn fund but simply as a share of revenue. Senior's later *Outline of the Science of Political Economy* has often been advanced as a prime example of the superficiality of this defence of the capitalist class, with its notions of the return to capital as a reward for the 'abstinence' or 'waiting' on the part of the capitalist. Despite the subjectivism that this entails, and which can be located at other points in the *Outline*, it must be emphasised that in attacking Classical Political Economy these writers were attempting to develop arguments that could deal with the economic issues of the day. The theories of distribution that Classical Political Economy embodied (and which were its achievement) could not provide any basis for arguments concerning wages and profits, as was shown in the attempt to provide them by J. S. Mill. It was therefore necessary to construct new conditions and principles, focusing on problems of time, price formation and the competition among heterogeneous capitals. The arguments which could be developed from these positions were in the first instance turned against the demands of the working class, who claimed that the worker who produced the object should receive the full value of the labour embodied. These arguments from the working-class movement were derived paradoxically from Classical Economics, such that the critique of Ricardo in the 1830s was carried out mainly *via* a critique of the Ricardian Socialists. However, the form in which the Ricardian system was presented in the debates between social classes was one which introduced into this system the very philosophical anthropology that Ricardo had rejected theoretically.

The so-called 'Ricardian Socialists' were writers such as Thompson, Hodgskin and Bray who adapted the Ricardian system into a defence of the rights of labour. This was effected through the introduction of a conception of property taken from Locke and combined with elements of utilitarianism, the latter particularly in the case of Thompson. In *An Inquiry into the Principles of the Distribution of Wealth most Conducive to Human Happiness*, the classical theory of distribution was taken up and projected on to a moral plane: 'The distribution to be here inquired into, is that which will promote the *greatest possible quantity* of human happiness, or the *greatest happiness of the greatest number*' (Thompson, 1824, p. 1). Wealth, claimed Thompson (1824, p. 35), is produced by labour, and the greatest stimulus to production that could be conceived was the securing to each labourer of the exclusive use of the products produced by that labourer. The failure to realise this will result in a lower average happiness in that society. The labourer thus becomes the real owner of everything by virtue of having produced it, and the utilitarian ethic of 'happiness' is used to describe the situation of optimum distribution of the products of labour. Capitalists can only exchange with labourers under condition that the exchange is a voluntary one and that the equivalent tendered by the capitalist is freely acknowledged by the labourer to be satisfactory (Thompson, 1824, p. 78). The economic concept of 'distribution' is thus reduced to a metaphor, the agents being constituted prior to and independent of this theory, and endowed with powers of decision which escape the sphere of the exchange relationship. Economic terminology is used by Thompson to construct a moral discourse, in which this terminology is invoked as a mode of proof of the rectitude of the moral positions put forward. The Ricardian Theory of distribution thus functions in this text as evidence for an argument which occupies a different discursive space.

Hodgskin (1825, p. 38) utilises economic terminology with more care, while sharing with Thompson the idea that the labourer is the 'real maker of the commodity', and as such entitled to the whole of the produce of labour. While the capitalists contribute fixed capital to the production process, this does not possess value because of its composition from previously stored-up labour: 'Fixed capital does not derive its utility from previous, but present labour; and does not bring its owner a profit because it has been stored up, but because it is a means of obtaining a command over labour' (1825, p. 55). Here in *Labour Defended against the Claims of Capital* the distribution of the product is determined according to the contribution of each class to the process of production. While capital is divided into two sections, fixed and circulating, the capitalist is not constituted as an economic agent, simply as a regulator of the sphere of production. The idea that the capitalist receives a revenue on the basis of his possession of means of production in the form of fixed capital is simply rejected; instead these means of production are placed in a discursive order as a means of domination rather than production. The inverse movement between profits and wages in the Classical System finds itself without the presence of any determinants other than the imperative of labour to the whole of the product: because the value of the product can be resolved entirely into labour, the labourers should receive the full value of this product as their 'wage'. The capitalist is left without any visible means of support, since in the exchanges that he does make he would, according to Hodgskin, simply be trading on behalf of the labourers. The theory of distribution that is proposed here is not so much one of *distribution* but of *flow* – from the purchaser straight into the pockets of the workers.

But of course there is a qualification to this schema, in which the capitalist receives his support from a relation which is external to this relation of distribution: the source of this revenue is the power of domination of the capitalist over the labourer, on the basis of which the capitalist is able to extort from the direct producers a portion of the product which is (rightfully) theirs. As in Thompson, the introduction of economic categories is deployed as a form of evidence in a moral argument, establishing the veracity of the moral analysis.

Capitalist and labourer are constituted as agents by Hodgskin not within a theory of production and distribution but according to the position of these agents with respect to economic property. In addition, this property can only be constituted as such by the action of the labourer, and so these agents are frozen in an eternal struggle in which the capitalist exists only to rob the worker of what is his. The support for this conception is derived from the work of Locke, and in the later *Natural and Artificial Rights of Property Contrasted*, lengthy quotation is made from chapter 5 of Book II of the *Two Treatises*. Hodgskin (1832,pp. 26–7) argues that the property of the subject is established by that subject mixing his labour with objects, so that the material property of the subject is a realisation of the property of the ability to labour:

> The power to labour is the gift of nature to each individual; and the power which belongs to each, cannot be confounded with that which belongs to another. The natural wants of man, particularly of food, are the natural stimulus to exert this power; and the means of gratifying them, which it provides, is the natural reward of the exertion. The power to labour and the natural wants which stimulate labour, are generally found together; thus we see that the motive to labour – the power to labour – and the produce of labour – all exist exclusive of legislation. Nature, not the legislator, creates man with these wants, and conjoins with them the power to gratify them.

Personal property in economic objects, the objects separated from Nature by that subject, is synonymous with the identity of the subject: 'It is as impossible for men not to have a notion of a right of property, as it is for them to want the idea of personal identity' (Hodgskin, 1832, p. 30); and it follows from this conception that the property of the subject is not alienable under the rights which such property establishes. Since the economic property of a subject is of the same order as his height or personality, to sell the products of his labour must be conceived here as equivalent to a sale of himself as a person. While it was shown in chapter 3 that such a mode of argument is a later construction on Locke, it can be seen how Hodgskin uses such a conception to argue that the process of exchange can only continue under a regime in which the capitalist dominates the labourer in the sphere of production.

It is the existence of a body of law (the 'artificial rights' of the title) that ensures the continuation of this process, overriding the Natural Law principles that are established discursively through the citation of Locke. Laws, argues Hodgskin, are made by others than the labourer, preserving the power of those who make them and enabling them to appropriate to themselves the products of others: 'In other words, the great object of law and goverment has been and is, to establish and protect a violation of that natural right of property they are described in theory as being intended to guarantee' (Hodgskin, 1832, p. 48). It is the possession of state power by the capitalists and landlords, and not their position as economic agents, that enables them to provide themselves with a revenue. The intervention of law undermines the natural rights established discursively, preventing the realisation of the state of affairs prescribed by Natural Law.

It is worth noting that this moral inflection of Ricardian theory, deploying this theory simply as evidence, has quite particular consequences for the political arguments that can be developed from it. By virtue of the postulated relation between the rights of labour and law, the restoration of the natural rights could only be effected by a destruction of the origin of these laws, the state. However, the very immensity of this prescribed task, confronting the state rather than the capitalists, guaranteed the inability of the workers to realise their liberation. The state had to be smashed at one blow, or not at all. The utopian nature of this requisite provided no alternative to this but a relapse into revolutionary rhetoric, continually denouncing the power of capital but impotent to oppose it effectively, except by issuing oppositional tracts or by engaging in sporadic and futile uprisings and riots.[3]

The restoration of Ricardian theory effected by the socialists was one which in the act of preservation simultaneously destroyed the theoretical rigour that had been the hallmark of Ricardo's work. Only with the long theoretical labour of Marx on the question of the nature of the capitalist economy would Ricardo's work be freed of the moralism which was the condition for the preservation of Ricardian theory in the 1830s and 1840s, a moralism which Marx of course himself shares wholeheartedly in his earlier writings. While Marx was to reject the humanism of the *1844 Manuscripts* which led him in that work to treat Ricardo as a cold-hearted apologist of the capitalist regime, the theoretical problems associated with the later use of conceptions of value and labour militated against a complete resolution of the difficulties that Marx faced. While the question of the relation between Ricardo and Marx has been a central one in the concerns of historians of economics for many years, it can be suggested that this seemingly clearcut relation, between two authors, between *Principles* and *Capital*, is a more complex one than usually thought, requiring for its exploration a radical re-assessment of the work of both authors.

8

Concluding Remarks

The writing of histories is an enterprise fraught with difficulties, difficulties that are apparently simplified by reliance on a chronology which offers the order that narrative imposes. 'History' provides a tempting pre-given chronology. The presence or absence of ideas, persons, things, books, places, and so on can be determined simply by reference to a discursive calendar – but unfortunately this involves more than basic organisational problems. The imbrication of history with chronology insinuates into the most well-meaning text the threat of turning time into a fundamental condition of existence of discourse, and in addition using the pervasive recurrence of a 'past' to construct a history teleologically. While the seventeenth- and eighteenth-century material presented in the preceding chapters is also the raw material of the histories of economics, it is in these histories constituted as the precursor and foundation of modern economic thought. In turn the dates of publication and lives of authors provides a pre-given succession to the progress of economic thought in which the fact of precedence becomes of itself a probable condition of existence.

By taking the categories 'land' and 'labour', categories which are universalised by modern economics as two of the three factors of production, an attempt has been made to reconsider the demands that historical discourse makes on these texts. The demonstration that these two apparently universal economic terms have no such unity, but are subject to the demands of the conceptual orders in which they are placed, both directs attention to the conditionality of these terms *qua* economic categories and disrupts the histories that economic analysis has constructed for itself. Thus while this book deals with archaic discursive forms, it cannot be said that it is historical; for the chronological foundation and the teleological construction typical of the history of economics does not form the organisational basis of the text.

At this level, then, I have tried to provide a methodological critique of the traditional approaches to the history of economic discourse, not through a detailed confrontation with the representatives of such history, but by a re-assessment of the material out of which they create their histories. Indeed, the rejection of philosophical and other modes of evaluation of discursive forms that is to be found in Chapter 1 naturally carries with it the implication that such methodological critiques can have only a strictly limited usefulness, one which is quite separate from the evaluation of economic discourse.

The arguments advanced in the preceding chapters are not, however, designed simply as a critique of one form of the history of ideas; they also seek to establish that the discursive eternalism ascribed to 'economics' is unfounded. Economic categories are not pre-given but have discursive and non-discursive conditions of existence. Thus such categories have no history; they are either (in one form or another) discursively present or discursively absent.

Further, the apparent centrality of the categories 'land' and 'labour' to the fact of human existence cannot be converted into the condition for the eternalism of economic thought. Only where Man is conceived as the constitutive element of the economy – where it is the action of this Man on external objects for the purpose of his preservation – can the terms 'land' and 'labour' be treated as such essential constituents of economic thought. The treatment of economics as universal and eternal thus relies on a humanism which obliterates and naturalises the specific conditions of existence of social forms. One of the purposes of this book is to demonstrate that such subjectivism obstructs the development of rigorous treatments of discursive forms.

The purpose of the arguments presented in the preceding chapters has been primarily to locate and clarify certain problems arising from the process of formation of economic discourse. However, the scope and length of this book necessitates a somewhat cursory treatment of major problems, although it is hoped that in such cases the allusions that are made suffice to indicate the nature of the problem and do not simply obscure the issue at hand. On the other hand, some comment is required on the manner in which authors and texts are dealt with in the preceding pages, for it could be suggested that the use of names and publications to signpost parts of the argument simply restores the historical method which has been explicitly rejected.

The use of authors and texts in this book is no more than a bibliographical device, enabling the reader to locate the terms and form of discussion as it proceeds. 'Smith' and 'Ricardo' are not treated as constitutive authorial subjects, intentionally setting in play a series of economic categories in the texts that they construct, and creating arguments which by virtue of their perceptiveness are coherent and logical. The evaluation of writing that takes place above addresses itself to the structure of specific texts, and does not invoke authorship as a means of analysis. However, it could further be objected that while eschewing the use of 'economic thought' to designate the terrain to be explored, a synonymous term is simply inserted – that of 'economic discourse'.

There are of course similarities between the usage here of 'economic discourse' and the 'archaeological unities' to be found in Foucault's *Order of Things*, unities which in their immanence appear and vanish in the order of discourse. Perhaps all that can be said at the moment is that such resonances, within the limitations of this text, are hard to avoid conclusively, and their reverberations are, it is hoped, limited by the specific arguments and material advanced in the substance of this book. On the other hand, it has been clearly stated at various points that 'economic discourse' is used to designate a discursive form that constitutes economic agents by means of theoretical statements concerning the production and distribution of commodities. Therefore, 'Classical Political Economy' is not a synonym for economic discourse, but is rather a realisation of it, and as such not reducible to, nor constitutive of, it.

It has also been demonstrated that discursive forms such as Classical Political Economy can be used as bases for the construction of political arguments, arguments which are themselves to an extent dependent on this discursive form but which are not invariantly related to it. Political statements may thus be linked to forms of economic discourse, but they are neither constitutive nor derivative of economic discourse. These three elements – economic discourse, its forms of realisation, and political argument – are independent entities and not reducible one to another; the presence of one in no way implicates the presence of another. The use of such epistemological terms as 'science' and 'ideology' in the evaluation of discourse implies such a conflation; while in the first case discourse, by virtue of its own powers of organisation, evades the sphere of the political, in the second case discourse can never escape the terrain of politics. The prior demarcation of discursive forms into these two sectors privileges the sciences and condemns ideological texts, introducing a discrepancy into the evaluation of texts which is inescapable. Such forms of epistemological analysis rely on a political teleology that has to be dispensed with if theoretical work is to develop.

Notes

Chapter 1 History and Discourse

1 I have discussed this problem in my paper, 'The "Histories" of Economic Discourse' (Tribe, 1977b). Many of the points raised in this chapter derive from this article.

2 Some of these discussions do sometimes degenerate to the level of an intellectual's who's who, as can be judged from this quotation from a not untypical text, Taylor's (1965, p. 59): 'While there is no trace in the works of David Hume of a discussion of the division of labour, additional anticipations of Smith's exposition are to be found in Sir William Petty's *Political Arithmetic* and Bernard de Mandeville's *Fable of the Bees*. The latter were particularly influential on Smith, and Dugald Stewart credited Mandeville with having been Smith's inspiration.'

3 See also Gordon (1966).

4 An extreme case of the recurrent mode of evaluation can be found in Allen's work (1968, pp. 74–5) on the Mercantilists, who are judged to be not 'real' economists because of their errors in the realm of price theory.

5 The reference here to the conventional literature is sketchy, but see, for example, Hartwell (1967), Hobsbawm (1969) and Landes (1969).

6 For a summary of the literature dealing with this problem, see Kindleberger (1976).

7 It will be shown in chapter 5 that if this conception of the division of labour is abandoned, and it is treated instead as a discursive element, completely different conclusions can be drawn concerning its place in the argument of *The Wealth of Nations*.

8 A detailed account of capitalist agrarian production can be found in chs 3, 4 and 5 of my doctoral dissertation (Tribe, 1976).

9 A typical example of the use to which Kuhn was put can be found in Meek's introduction to his selection *Precursors of Adam Smith* (1973, pp. vii–xv). The specificity of Smithian political economy is related here to the 'paradigmatic' character of Smith's work. Coats (1969, p. 292) has also suggested that Kuhn provides a 'new interpretive framework'. Other discussions can be found in Collard (1972) and Stanfield (1974).

10 For a more detailed critique, see Tribe (1973).

11 For a lucid introduction to the work of Bachelard, see Gaukroger (1976). Also, Hirst (1975) relies heavily on Bachelard's work, albeit orientated to a science/non-science form of distinction. See especially the discussion of Bernard's notion of internal milieu (1975, pp. 64 ff.). The use of Bachelard here should not be taken as a simple endorsement of the results of his work – criticism can be levelled at a number of his key categories.

12 Another exemplary example is Clavelin (1974.). A brief summary of the merits of the text can be found in Counihan (1976). Mention must also be made here of the work of Foucault, whose writings are not directly discussed in this introductory chapter; see particularly *The Birth of the Clinic, The Order of Things* and *The Archaeology of Knowledge*.

Chapter 2 'Rent' as an Economic Category

1 For a discussion of this, see my doctoral dissertation (Tribe, 1976, ch. 2.2 and 2.6).

2 The following account is simply an outline of economic relations pertinent to a discussion of the term 'rent' in agrarian economies organised on the basis of serf labour. It is neither exhaustive nor complete, and is based on the accounts provided by Maitland's *Domesday Book and Beyond*, Milsom's *Historical Foundations of the Common Law*, Pollock and Maitland's *History of English Law* and Postan's *Medieval Economy and Society*.

3 Of course on the Continent there was allodial land outside this structure (Simpson, 1961, pp. 2–3), as well as tenants of Ancient Demesne in England who held directly of the king.

4 Gurevich (1977, pp. 8–9) has argued that this opposition of Man to Nature is a notion that emerged later, for in the Middle Ages men traced their attributes in the cosmos and did not precisely distinguish the world of objects from the world of men.

Chapter 3 Property, Patriarchy and the Constitution of a Polity

1 An alternative mode of criticism could be to argue that Macpherson's assumption that the seventeenth-century economy was a 'market society', i.e. dominated by capitalist relations, is not supported by historical evidence. While this could in fact be sustained, it would simply reproduce the error of supposing that a non-discursive form (an economy) conditions a discursive form in such a way that reference from the latter to the former is considered an adequate form of explanation and proof.

2 It is worth emphasising here that by 'household' we do not mean 'persons living under the same roof' but 'persons included under the authority of one head'. The conception of household as the former has led Laslett (1964, p. 152) to make spurious criticisms of Macpherson. Schochet (1975, ch. iv) himself assumes that 'patriarchal families' are a necessary condition for a theory of patriarchy.

3 Macpherson's book was heralded at its publication as a major work of

re-interpretation of seventeenth-century thought. See the adulatory review
by Hill, for example (1963).

4 It must be added that this criticism does not apply to Macpherson's
treatment of the Levellers, for precisely in this chapter of *Possessive
Individualism* the question is the criteria for political enfranchisement, that
is, the constitution of political agents. Macpherson argues against the
popular view of the Levellers as *avant-garde* democrats on the basis of the
different schemes of political representation that they proposed. He is able to
show that even the most open franchise would have fallen a long way short
of manhood suffrage. But what is disconcerting is that this serious
consideration of the Leveller construct of 'man' is not matched elsewhere in
the book.

5 Thus 'Fictive personality' is not, as in Roman Law, a device for giving
personality to inanimate objects, but is used by Hobbes to refer to the
function of representation of words and actions in general. When the term
'fiction' is used this does not denote 'untrue' or 'false'; it means 'artificial',
requiring authority from elsewhere for the words and actions to be
authoritative. This 'elsewhere' is another man, not simply another legal
personality. This is clear from the discussion of contracts between actors:
'And therefore he that maketh a Covenant with the Actor, or Representer,
not knowing the Authority he hath, doth it at his own perill. For no man is
obliged by a Covenant, whereof he is not Author; nor consequently by a
Covenant made against, or beside the Authority he gave' (Hobbes, 1968, p.
218).

6 The summary of Locke's treatment of property is relatively cursory, and is
heavily indebted to Jim Tully's painstaking treatment of Locke in his thesis
'John Locke's Writings on Property in the Seventeenth Century Intellectual
Context'.

7 What man owns is not his life but his person (Tully, 1977, pp. 133–4). In the
example that follows, the thief seeks to steal the *person*, i.e. the possessions
and faculties of man.

8 Tully emphasises that this right to land in the state of nature is a right of use,
i.e. to products, and not a right to alienate the land. The right of property
involving such alienation (private dominion) is expounded by Filmer, not
Locke. It must be stressed that 'property' does not necessarily entail rights of
alienation; this was true of the seventeenth century in general, and Locke in
particular (Tully, 1977, p. 127, fn. 14).

Chapter 4 The Agricultural Treatise 1600–1800

1 Particularly important in that this period marks the transition from quit-rent
to capitalist ground-rent (see Laurence, 1726, ch. II).

2 This derives from the philosophy of earth expounded by Evelyn (1706).

3 The defenders of small farms consistently treated them within a framework
of landlord–tenant relations, thus taking for granted that it was small
tenancies that were at issue. Nowhere does the advocacy of the small farmer
rest on a defence of owner-occupiers. This point has to be stressed because

of the tendency among agrarian historians to associate small farms with owner-occupancy (Chambers and Mingay, 1966, pp. 88–96).

Chapter 5 The Structure of Political Oeconomy

1 As was shown in the previous chapter, the seventeenth-century agricultural treatise can be described as a *husbandry* tract, while that of the eighteenth century is a *farming* tract. An interesting comparison is made by Singer (1958, p. 34) with the German term *Wirtschaft*, which in old German denoted a rural household under the control of a master, *wirtschaften* and *husbanding* carrying the same meaning. But while the English term became narrowed to the simple conception of master in a marriage relation, the German term moved first to the designation of a place of hospitality, such as an inn, and today is the bearer of *oikonomia* as the equivalent of the English 'economy'. It is also worth noting that there still exists in modern German another term for 'economy' which is *Ökonomie*, derived directly from the Greek, but this is little used on account of its alien derivation.

2 On this point see the discussion in Barber (1975).

3 A comparison can be made with Hume's (1955, p. 85) comments on 'good' and 'bad' taxes.

4 This is the basis of the nineteenth-century humanist analysis of economic activity that Rancière outlined in his investigation of the writings of the Young Marx. He shows how in this discourse a series of transpositions are made from the terminology of Classical Political Economy, such that 'worker' is read as 'man', 'labour' as 'generic activity', 'means of subsistence' as 'means of life', and so forth. The form in which this operates is described as follows (Rancière, 1971, p. 42):

> Man produces God, i.e. he objectifies in God the predicates which make up his essence. So now when we say that the worker *produces* an object, we start from the prosaic concept of production, but the slide takes place thanks to this concept which enables us to think of the relationship between the worker and his product on the model of the relation between God and man in religion. So the productive activity is identified with the generic activity (the activity of man in so far as he affirms his own essence) and the object produced is identified with the objectification of the generic being of man. The fact that this product should go to increase the power of Capital then appears as the final stage of alienation, that in which man becomes the object of his object.

5 This is exemplified in Corn Law legislation prior to 1660, which was aimed at the practices of forestalling, regrating and engrossing. These were respectively: dealing before corn reached the market in order to enhance the price; buying in one market in order to sell in another at a higher price; buying or contracting to buy grain before it had been harvested with the intention of reselling (see Barnes, 1930, p. 2).

6 However, as will be suggested below this does not mean that the economic forms sketched by the Physiocrats are 'capitalist', nor that their discourse

can be said to have as a referent a 'capitalist reality'.
7 Hume (1955, p. 11) states that:

> Every thing in the world is purchased by labour; and our passions are the
> only causes of labour. When a nation abounds in manufactures and
> mechanic arts, the proprietors of land, as well as the farmers, study
> agriculture as a science, and redouble their industry and attention. The
> superfluity, which arises from their labour, is not lost; but is exchanged
> with manufactures for those commodities, which men's luxury now
> makes them covet. By this means, land furnishes a great deal more of the
> necessaries of life, than what suffices for those who cultivate it.

Note that finally 'the land furnishes' the surplus, not labour.
8 This is emphasised by Foucault (1970, p. 194), where he argues that rent is
  crucial for the Physiocrats because it is the gift of God which permits the
  functioning of the economy.
9 The accuracy of Lüthy's observations concerning Physiocracy derives from
  his extensive research into seventeenth- and eighteenth-century finance, a
  matter which is at the heart of the economies of the time. In seeking to
  understand the complexities of activities and legislation he was necessarily
  brought to the conjunction of theology and circulation which underpinned
  these processes. Fox-Genovese (1976, p. 293) criticises him for under-
  estimating the 'capitalist' character of Physiocracy, but the accuracy of
  Lüthy's presentation is a direct outcome of his immersion in the raw
  material of the crisis of the French economy.
10 A similar problem to the one outlined here arises in the translation of terms
  like 'value' and 'price' in Meek's *Economics of Physiocracy*. In general the
  translation tends to improve on the original by removing what might appear
  to be inconsistent synonyms. Note, for example, the following passage
  (Meek, 1962, p. 74; my italics):

> In this case a nation draws from its land and its men the maximum
> product which can be drawn from them; but it gains much more from
> the sale of a million livres worth of manufactured commodities, because
> in the case of the latter it gains only the *value* of the artisan's labour,
> whereas in the case of the former it gains the *value* of the labour of
> cultivation and also the *value* of the materials produced by the *land*.

The original in fact uses the term *prix* where 'value' is italicised above, and
the original for the final word is *sol*, not *terre*. These are small differences
perhaps, but none the less significant, for the translation tends in this way to
impose a modernity and consistency not present in the original. Meek is of
course sensitive to the way in which Quesnay (1958, vol. II, pp. 526–7)
changes the terms used for apparently synonymous notions – for example,
in his 'Hommes' the series 'venal price', 'alimentary price', 'commercial
value' and 'usual value' all appear – and he in fact discusses such difficulties
in his Introductuion (Meek, 1962, p. 41).
11 My article, 'The "Histories" of Economic Discourse' (Tribe, 1977b) covers
  some of the ground to be found in this chapter, but contains some additional
  points that are related to the argument here.

Chaper 6 The Formation of Economic Discourse

1 For a more detailed treatment of these early nineteenth-century texts, see the essay by Meek entitled 'Physiocracy and Classicism in Britain', in his *Economics of Physiocracy*.

2 To simplify matters somewhat, and disregarding the effect of Corn Law legislation, which operated to prevent imports below certain prices, farmers received their greatest revenue when prices were high and the crop below average. A 'good year' for a farmer was a 'bad year' for consumers of his products and vice versa. However, the rent paid per acre was an expression of this, and the landlords consequently reaped the long-term benefits from high prices. During the Napoleonic wars there was a great increase in the extent of arable farming, and rent levels rose accordingly. Failure to pay the higher rents on the part of tenants resulted in land becoming derelict, the typical form of a capitalist agricultural crisis.

3 The form of such popular disturbances and their relation to the circulation of agricultural goods is discussed by Rose (1961), Shelton (1973) and Stevenson (1974). E. P. Thompson (1971, p. 108) shows how these disturbances embodied conceptions of the 'just price' although it must be stressed that the rise of selling by sample and bulk dealing meant that the established mechanisms of marketing and distribution increasingly displaced the local and regional market-place as a significant institution (see Chartres, 1973, pp. 67–9).

4 The following passages are taken from my 'Economic Property and the Theorisation of Ground Rent' (Tribe, 1977a).

5 The shift from *Essay* to *Principles* with respect to the conditionality of agrarian production is discussed later in this chapter.

6 A discussion of the changes in Malthus's *Essay on Population* in succeeding editions can be found in Flew's Introduction to the Penguin edition (1970, pp. 13–31).

7 Compare this passage with the first paragraph of *The Wealth of Nations*: the latter is more amenable to 'modernistic' reading than the former.

8 See the discussion later in the chapter of the use made by political economists of the term 'value'.

9 Compare the order of Malthus's *Principles of Political Economy* of 1820:
Book I ch. 1: On the Definitions of Wealth and Productive Labour
    ch. 2: On the Nature and Measures of Value
    ch. 3: Of the Rent of Land
    ch. 4: Of the Wages of Labour
    ch. 5: Of the Profits of Capital
    ch. 6: Of the Distinction between Wealth and Value
    ch. 7: On the Immediate Causes of the Progress of Wealth
It can be seen that the order of problems follows that laid down by Smith, in particular in associating wealth and labour, an association absent in Ricardo.

10 While revising *Principles* for the second edition, Ricardo, in response to criticism from Torrens, formulated a distinction of fixed from circulating capital which did not rest on time of circulation, but rather on the distinction of the property of the capitalist from that of the labourer. Accordingly, fixed capital denoted all raw materials and finished goods contributing to

production minus wages, and circulating capital was equated with wages alone (Ricardo 1951, vol. IV, pp. 311–12). Essentially this distinction is the same as that formulated by Ramsay in his *Essay on the Distribution of Wealth* and corresponds of course to Marx's distinction between constant and variable capital.

11 The connection between an agrarian-based theory of gluts and the existence of luxury consumers can be seen in Chalmers (1832, pp. 40–6). He argued that a third class (in addition to the agricultural class and the producers of necessaries) of labour arises, one of luxury producers, whose task is to work up into goods the surplus produce of the land. This tripartite distinction underwrites automatically the position of landlords as unproductive consumers.

Chapter 7 The Dissolution of Classical Political Economy

1 Because the accounts of Political Oeconomy and Classical Political Economy do not depend on the existence of a grid for their realisation, it is possible to account for the regularity of their respective organisations while opposing to these accounts the alternative modes of critique which 'dissolve' the organisation of these structures. For example, it was possible to demonstrate the rationality of 'Physiocracy' and then show how Smith's mode of critique reduced this rationality to incoherence. If Classical Political Economy had been constructed as a 'predecessor' or 'forerunner', it would not have been possible to show how it was rendered obsolete in the attempt to utilise its theoretical statements under conditions not given in the original discursive form.

2 For a survey of Marx's comments on these writers, see Maxine Berg (1975), which draws together the various remarks that were made on the writers of the 1830s and 1840s.

3 An example of such a revolutionary tract is Bray's *Labour's Wrongs and Labour's Remedy*, where it is maintained that universal suffrage or the establishment of a republic would not be sufficient condition for the achievement of a just society. The perpetual opposition of capital and labour was irreconcilable, and could only be ended by the sweeping away of the basis of the capitalist's power – the state (Bray, 1839, pp. 60–1).

Bibliography

Allen, W. R. (1968), 'The Position of Mercantilism and the Early Development of International Trade Theory', in R. V. Eagly (ed.), *Events, Ideology and Economic Theory*, Wayne State University Press, Detroit, pp. 65–106.

Anderson, James (1777), *Observations on the Means of Exciting a Spirit of National Industry*, Edinburgh.

Anderson, James (1801), *Recreations in Agriculture, Natural-History, Arts, and Miscellaneous Literature*, vol. V, London.

Anstruther, J. (1796), *Remarks on the Drill Husbandry*, London.

Bachelard, G. (1964), *The Psychoanalysis of Fire*, Beacon Press, Boston.

Bachelard, G. (1965), *L'Activité Rationaliste de la physique contemporaine*, 2nd ed., PUF, Paris.

Bachelard, G. (1970), *La Formation de l'esprit scientifique*, 7th ed., Vrin, Paris.

Bailey, S. (1825), *A Critical Dissertation on the Nature, Measure, and Causes of Value*, Hunter, London.

Baker, J. W. (1764), *A New Plan for more effectually Propagating the Knowledge of Husbandry, in the Kingdom of Ireland, and reducing it to a Rational and Intelligible System*, Dublin.

Barber, W. J. (1967), *A History of Economic Thought*, Penguin, Harmondsworth.

Barber, W. J. (1975), *British Economic Thought and India 1600–1858*, Oxford University Press, London.

Barnes, D. G. (1930), *A History of the English Corn Laws 1600–1846*, George Routledge, London.

Barnett, G. E. (ed.) (1936), *Two Tracts by Gregory King*, Johns Hopkins Press, Baltimore.

Barton, J. (1817), *Observations on the Circumstances which Influence the Condition of the Labouring Classes of Society*, London.

Berg, M. (1975), 'Vulgar Economy and Ricardo's Critics', *Bulletin of the Conference of Socialist Economists*, 4 (3), MB1–15.

Black, R. D. C., Coats, A. W. and **Goodwin, C. D. W.** (eds) (1973), *The Marginal Revolution in Economics*, Duke University Press, Durham, N.C.

Blagrave, J. (1675), *The Epitome of the Whole Art of Husbandry*, London.

Blaug, M. (1968), *Economic Theory in Retrospect*, 2nd ed., Heinemann, London.

Blaug, M. (1976), 'Kuhn versus Lakatos *or* Paradigms versus Research

Programmes in the History of Economics', in S. J. Latsis (ed.), *Method and Appraisal in Economics*, Cambridge University Press, 1976, pp. 149–80.

Blith, W. (1652), *The English Improver Improved, or the Survey of Husbandry Surveyed*, London.

Bodin, J. (n.d.), *Six Books of the Commonwealth* (trans. and abridged M. J. Tooley), Blackwell, Oxford.

Boileau, D. (1811), *An Introduction to the Study of Political Economy*, London.

Bradley, R. (1727), *A Complete Body of Husbandry; Collected From the Practice and Experience of the Most Considerable Farmers in Britain*, London.

Bray, J. F. (1839), *Labour's Wrongs and Labour's Remedy*, David Green, Leeds.

Bronfenbrenner, M. (1970), 'The "Structure of Revolutions" in Economic Thought', *History of Political Economy*, vol. 2, pp. 136–51.

Buchanan, D. (1814), *Observations on the Subjects treated of in Dr Smith's Inquiry into the Nature and Causes of the Wealth of Nations*, Oliphant, Waugh & Innes, Edinburgh.

Calthrope, C. (1635), *The Relation betweene the Lord of a Mannor and the Coppy-Holder his Tenant*, William Cooke, London.

Canguilhem, G. (1955), *La Formation du concept de réflexe aux XVIIᵉ et XVIIIᵉ siècles*, PUF, Paris.

Cantillon, R. (1959), *Essai sur la nature du commerce en général*, Frank Cass, London.

Cardwell, D. S. L. (1972), 'Science and the Steam Engine, 1790–1825', in P. Mathias (ed.), *Science and Society 1600–1900*, Cambridge University Press, pp. 81–96.

Cato and Varro (1934), *On Agriculture* (trans. W. D. Hooper and H. B. Ash), Harvard University Press, Cambridge, Mass.

Chalmers, T. (1832), *On Political Economy in connection with the Moral State and Moral Prospects of Society*, 2nd ed., Collins, Glasgow.

Chambers, J. D. and Mingay, G. E. (1966), *The Agricultural Revolution*, Batsford, London.

Chapman, S. D. (1974), 'The Textile Factory before Arkwright: A Typology of Factory Development', *Business History Review*, 48, pp. 451–77.

Chartres, J. (1973), 'Markets and Marketing in Metropolitan Western England in the Late Seventeenth and Eighteenth Centuries', in M. Havinden (ed.), *Husbandry and Marketing in the South-West, 1500–1800*, Exeter Papers in Economic History, no. 8, pp. 63–74.

Clarke, C. (1777), *The True Theory and Practice of Husbandry: Deduced from Philosophical Researches, and Experience*, London.

Clavelin, M. (1974), *The Natural Philosophy of Galileo*, MIT Press.

Clerke, G. (1728), *The Landed Man's Assistant: or, the Stewards Vade Mecum*, Dublin.

Coats, A. W. (1969), 'Is there a "Structure of Scientific Revolutions" in Economics?', *Kyklos*, 22, pp. 289–95.

Collard, D. (1972), 'Paradigms and the Historian of Economic Thought', *History of Economic Thought Newsletter*, no. 8, pp. 10–13.

Columella (1948–55), *On Agriculture* (trans. H. B. Ash, E. S. Forster and E. H. Heffner) (3 vols), Heinemann, London.

Counihan, T. (1976), 'Epistemology of Science – Feyerabend and Lecourt',

Economy and Society, 5, pp. 74–110.

Crouzet, F. (1972), Editor's Introduction in F. Crouzet (ed.), *Capital Formation in the Industrial Revolution*, Methuen, London, pp. 1–69.

D'avenant, C. (1771), *The Political and Commercial Works of that Celebrated Writer Charles D'avenant, L.L.D.*, 5 vols, London.

Duby, G. (1968), *Rural Economy and Country Life in the Medieval West*, Edward Arnold, London.

Eagly, R. V. (1974), *The Structure of Classical Economic Theory*, Oxford University Press, New York.

Ernle, Lord (1961), *English Farming, Past and Present*, 6th ed., Heinemann and Frank Cass, London.

Estienne, C. (1606), *Maison Rustique, or The Countrey Farme*, London.

Evelyn, J. (1706), *Terra. A Philosophical Discourse of Earth. Appended to 4th ed. of Silva, or a Discourse of Forest-Trees, and the Propagation of Timber*, London.

Feigl, H. (1974), 'Empiricism at Bay?', in R. S. Cohen and M. W. Wartofsky (eds), *Methodological and Historical Essays in the Natural and Social Sciences*, Boston Studies in the Philosophy of Science, vol. 14, Reidel, Dordrecht, pp. 1–20.

Filmer, R. (1949), *Patriarcha and other Political Works of Sir Robert Filmer* (ed. and introduced by P. Laslett), Blackwell, Oxford.

Finley, M. I. (1970), 'Aristotle and Economic Analysis', *Past and Present*, no. 47, pp. 3–25.

Fitzherbert, J. (1882), *The Book of Husbandry*, Trübner, London.

Flew, A. (1970), Introduction to Malthus (1970a).

Foucault, M. (1970), *The Order of Things*, Tavistock, London.

Foucault, M. (1972), *The Archaeology of Knowledge*, Tavistock, London.

Foucault, M. (1973), *The Birth of the Clinic*, Tavistock, London.

Fox-Genovese, E. (1976), *The Origins of Physiocracy*, Cornell University Press, Ithaca.

Fussell, G. E. (1947), *The Old English Farming Books from Fitzherbert to Tull*, Crosby Lockwood, London.

Gaukroger, S. W. (1976), 'Bachelard and the Problem of Epistemological Analysis', *Studies in the History and Philosophy of Science*, 7, pp. 189–244.

Gordon, B. (1966), 'W. F. Lloyd: A Neglected Contribution', *Oxford Economic Papers*, new series, 18, pp. 64–70.

Gordon, B. (1967), *Non-Ricardian Political Economy*, Harvard Graduate School of Business Administration, Boston.

Gordon, D. F. (1965), 'The Role of the History of Economic Thought in the Understanding of Modern Economic Theory', *American Economic Review*, 55, Papers and Proceedings, pp. 119–27.

Gurevich, A. (1977), 'Representations of Property during the High Middle Ages', *Economy and Society*, 6, pp. 1–30.

Hale, T. (1758), *A Compleat Body of Husbandry*, 4 vols, 2nd ed., London.

Harte, W. (1764), *Essays on Husbandry*, London.

Hartlib, S. (1651), *The Reformed Husband-man*, London.

Hartwell, R. M. (ed.) (1967), *The Causes of the Industrial Revolution in England*, Methuen, London.

Heaton, H. (1972), 'Financing the Industrial Revolution', in F. Crouzet (ed.),

Capital Formation in the Industrial Revolution, Methuen, London, pp. 84–93.

Hill, C. (1963), 'Possessive Individualism', *Past and Present*, no. 24, pp. 86–9.

Hilton, R. H. (1947), *The Economic Development of some Leicestershire Estates in the 14th and 15th Centuries*, Oxford University Press, London.

Hindess, B. (1977), *Philosophy and Methodology in the Social Sciences*, Harvester Press, Brighton.

Hirst, P. Q. (1975), *Durkheim, Bernard and Epistemology*, Routledge & Kegan Paul, London.

Hitt, T. (1760), *A Treatise of Husbandry on the Improvement of Dry and Barren Lands*, Richardson, London.

Hobbes, T. (1968), *Leviathan*, Penguin, Harmondsworth.

Hobbes, T. (1971), *A Dialogue between a Philosopher and a Student of the Laws of England*, University of Chicago Press.

Hobsbawm, E. J. (1968), *Industry and Empire*, Wiedenfeld & Nicolson, London.

Hodgskin, T. (1825), *Labour Defended against the Claims of Capital*, Knight & Lacey, London.

Hodgskin, T. (1832), *The Natural and Artificial Rights of Property Contrasted*, Steil, London.

Hollander, S. (1973), *The Economics of Adam Smith*, Heinemann, London.

Horner, F. (1803), 'Canard's "Principes d'économie politique" ', *Edinburgh Review*, 1 (2), pp. 431–50.

Hume, D. (1955), *Writings on Economics* (ed. E. Rotwein), Nelson, London.

Jacob, G. (1717), *The Country Gentleman's Vade Mecum*, London.

Johnson, E. A. J. (1937), *Predecessors of Adam Smith*, P. S. King, London.

Kent, N. (1796), *General View of the Agriculture of the County of Norfolk; with Observations for the Means of its Improvement*, George Nicol, London.

Kindleberger, C. (1976), 'The Historical Background: Adam Smith and the Industrial Revolution', in T. S. Wilson and A. S. Skinner (eds), *The Market and the State*, Oxford University Press, London, pp. 1–25.

King, G. (1936), 'Natural and Political Observations and Conclusions upon the State and Condition of England (1696)', in G. E. Barnett (ed.), *Two Tracts by Gregory King*, Johns Hopkins Press, Baltimore.

Kosminsky, E. A. (1956), *Studies in the Agrarian History of England in the Thirteenth Century*, Blackwell, Oxford.

Kuhn, T. S. (1970), *The Structure of Scientific Revolutions*, 2nd ed., University of Chicago Press.

Kula, W. (1976), *An Economic Theory of the Feudal System*, New Left Books, London.

Kunin, L. and **Weaver, F. S.** (1971), 'On the Structure of Scientific Revolutions in Economics', *History of Political Economy*, 3, pp. 391–7.

Lakatos, I. (1970), 'Falsification and the Methodology of Scientific Research Programmes', in I. Lakatos and A Musgrave (eds), *Criticism and the Growth of Knowledge*, Cambridge University Press, pp. 91–196.

Lakatos, L. (1971), 'History of Science and its Rational Reconstructions', in R. C. rBuck and R. S. Cohen (eds), *Boston Studies in the Philosophy of Science*, 8, Reidel, Dordrecht, pp. 91–136.

Landes, D. (1969), *The Unbound Prometheus*, Cambridge University Press.

Laslett, P. (1949), Introduction to Filmer (1949), pp. 1–48.

Laslett, P. (1964), 'Market Society and Political Theory', *Historical Journal*, 7, pp. 150–4.

Latsis, S. J. (1972), 'Situational Determinism in Economics', *British Journal for the Philosophy of Science*, 23, pp. 207–45.

Latsis, S. J. (ed.) (1976), *Method and Appraisal in Economics*, Cambridge University Press.

Lauderdale, Earl of (1804), *An Inquiry into the Nature and Origin of Public Wealth, and into the Means and Causes of its Increase*, Constable, Edinburgh.

Laurence, E. (1727), *The Duty of a Steward to His Lord*, London.

Laurence, J. (1726), *A New System of Agriculture: Being a Complete Body of Husbandry and Gardening*, London.

Lawrence, J. (1786), *The Modern Land Steward*, 2nd ed., London.

Lecourt, D. (1972), *Pour une critique de l'épistémologie*, Maspéro, Paris.

Letwin, W. (1963), *The Origins of Scientific Economics*, Methuen, London.

Lewis, J. (1772), *Uniting and Monopolising Farms, Plainly proved disadvantageous to the Land-Owners, and highly prejudicial to the Public*, 2nd ed., Ipswich.

Locke, J. (1960), *Two Treatises of Government* (ed. P. Laslett), Cambridge University Press.

Longfield, M. (1834), *Lectures on Political Economy*, Milliken, Dublin.

Lublinskaya, A. D. (1968), *French Absolutism*, Cambridge University Press.

Lüthy, H. (1970), *From Calvin to Rousseau*, Basic Books, New York.

McCulloch, J. R. (1821), 'The Opinions of Messrs. Say, Sismondi, and Malthus, on Effects of Machinery and Accumulation', *Edinburgh Review*, 35, pp. 102–23.

McDonald, D. (1908), *Agricultural Writers, from Sir Walter of Henley to Arthur Young, 1200–1800*, Horace Cox, London.

McKendrick, N. (1961), 'Josiah Wedgwood and Factory Discipline', *Historical Journal*, 4, pp. 30–55.

Macpherson, C. B. (1962), *The Political Theory of Possessive Individualism*, Oxford University Press, London.

Macpherson, C. B. (1965), 'Hobbes's Bourgeois Man', in K. C. Brown (ed.), *Hobbes Studies*, Blackwell, Oxford, pp. 169–83.

Macpherson, C. B. (1968), Introduction to T. Hobbes, *Leviathan*, Penguin, Harmondsworth.

Maitland, F. W. (1907), *Domesday Book and Beyond*, Cambridge University Press.

Malthus, T. R. (1820), *Principles of Political Economy*, John Murray, London.

Malthus, T. R. (1823), *The Measure of Value Stated and Illustrated*, John Murray, London.

Malthus, T. R. (1836), *Principles of Political Economy*, 2nd ed., William Pickering, London.

Malthus, T. R. (1970a), *An Essay on the Principles of Population*, Penguin, Harmondsworth.

Malthus, T. R. (1970b), *The Pamphlets of Thomas Robert Malthus*, Kelley, New York.

Marshall, W. (1778), *Minutes of Agriculture*, Dodsley, London.

Marshall, W. (1808), *The Review and Abstract of the County Reports to the Board of Agriculture*, vol, I, Longman and others, London.

Marx, K. (1959), *Economic and Philosophic Manuscripts of 1844*, Progress Publishers, Moscow.

Meager, L. (1697), *The Mystery of Husbandry: or Arable, Pasture and Woodland Improved*, London.

Meek, R. L. (1962), *The Economics of Physiocracy*, Allen & Unwin, London.

Meek, R. L. (1973), *Precursors of Adam Smith*, Dent, London.

Mill, J. (1966), *Selected Economic Writings* (ed. D. Winch), Oliver & Boyd, Edinburgh.

Mill, J. S. (1844), *Essays on Some Unsettled Questions of Political Economy*, J. W. Parker, London.

Mills, J. (1762–7), *A New and Complete System of Practical Husbandry*, 5 vols, London.

Milsom, S. F. C. (1969), *Historical Foundations of the Common Law*, Butterworths, London.

Mordant, J. (1761), *The Complete Steward: or, the Duty of a Steward to his Lord*, 2 vols, London.

Mortimer, J. (1707), *The Whole Art of Husbandry: Or, the Way of Managing and Improving of Land*, London.

Mossé, C. (1969), *The Ancient World at Work*, Chatto & Windus, London.

Musson, A. E. and **Robinson, E.** (1969), *Science and Technology in the Industrial Revolution*, Manchester University Press.

Norden, J. (1618), *The Surveior's Dialogue*, London.

O'Brien, D. P. (1976), 'The Longevity of Adam Smith's Vision: Paradigms, Research Programmes and Falsifiability in the History of Economic Thought', *Scottish Journal of Political Economy*, 23, pp. 133–51.

Osier, J.-P. (1976), *Thomas Hodgskin: Une critique prolétarienne de l'économie politique*, Maspéro, Paris.

Petty, W. (1899), *The Economic Writings of Sir William Petty*, 2 vols, (ed. C. H. Hull), Cambridge University Press.

Pocock, J. G. A. (1957), *The Ancient Constitution and the Feudal Law*, Cambridge University Press.

Political Economy Club (1921), *Centenary Volume: Minutes of Proceedings*, vol. 6, Macmillan, London.

Pollard, S. (1965), *The Genesis of Modern Management*, Edward Arnold, London.

Pollock, F. and **Maitland, F. W.** (1968), *The History of English Law before the Time of Edward I*, 2 vols, 2nd ed. (introduced S. F. C. Milsom), Cambridge University Press.

Popper, K. (1969), *Conjectures and Refutations*, 3rd ed., Routledge & Kegan Paul, London.

Postan, M. (1972), *Medieval Economy and Society*, Weidenfeld & Nicolson, London.

Purves, G. (1817), *All Classes Productive of National Wealth*, Longman and others, London.

Quesnay, F. (1958), *François Quesnay et la Physiocratie*, 2 vols, INED, Paris.

Quesnay, F. (1972), *Tableau Economique* (ed. M. Kuczynski and R. L. Meek), Macmillan, London.

Ramsay, G. (1836), *An Essay on the Distribution of Wealth*, Adam and Charles Black, Edinburgh.

Rancière, J. (1971), 'The Concept of "Critique" and the "Critique of Political Economy": Pt I', *Theoretical Practice*, no. 1, pp. 35–52.

Ricardo, D. (1951–2), *Works and Correspondence*, vols I–IX (ed. P. Sraffa and M. H. Dobb), Cambridge University Press.

Robertson, T. (1796), *Outline of the General Report on the Size of Farms*, Edinburgh.

Roll, E. (1954), *A History of Economic Thought*, 3rd ed., Faber & Faber, London.

Rose, R. B. (1961), 'Eighteenth Century Price Riots and Public Policy in England', *International Review of Social History*, 4, pp. 277–92.

Say, J. B. (1821), 'Letters of Mr. Malthus, on Various Subjects of Political Economy', *Pamphleteer*, vol. 17, no. 34, pp. 289–345.

Schochet, G. J. (1975), *Patriarchalism in Political Thought*, Blackwell, Oxford.

Senior, N. W. (1830), *Three Lectures on the Rate of Wages*, John Murray, London.

Senior, N. W. (1938), *An Outline of the Science of Political Economy*, Allen & Unwin, London.

Shelton, W. J. (1973), *English Hunger and Industrial Disorders*, Macmillan, London.

Simpson, A. W. B. (1961), *An Introduction to the History of Land Law*, Oxford University Press, London.

Singer, K. (1958), 'Oikonomia: An Enquiry into the Beginnings of Economic Thought and Language', *Kyklos*, 11, pp. 29–54.

Skinner, A. S. and **Wilson, T.** (1975), *Essays on Adam Smith*, Oxford University Press, London.

Smart, W. (1970), *Economic Annals of the Nineteenth Century, 1801–1820*, Macmillan, London.

Smith, A. (1802), *Recherches sur la nature et les causes de la richesse des nations* (ed. G. Garnier), 5 vols, Agasse, Paris.

Smith, A. (1814), *An Inquiry into the Nature and Causes of the Wealth of Nations* (ed. D. Buchanan), 3 vols, Oliphant, Waugh & Innes, Edinburgh.

Smith, A. (1828), *An Inquiry into the Nature and Causes of the Wealth of Nations* (ed. J. R. McCulloch), 4 vols, Black & Tait, Edinburgh.

Smith, A. (1896), *Lectures on Justice, Police, Revenue and Arms* (ed. E. Cannan), Kelley & Milman, New York.

Smith, A. (1970), *The Wealth of Nations* (ed. A. S. Skinner), Penguin, Harmondsworth.

Smith, A. (1976), An Inquiry into the Nature and Causes of the Wealth of Nations (ed. R. H. Campbell and A. S. Skinner), 2 vols, Oxford University Press, London.

Smith, T. (1906), *De Republica Anglorum* (ed. L. Alston), Cambridge University Press.

Speed, A. (1659), *Adam out of Eden: Or, An Abstract of Divers Excellent Experiments Touching the Advancement of Husbandry*, London.

Spence, W. (1822), *Tracts on Political Economy*, Longman and others, London.

Sraffa, P. (1951), Introduction to D. Ricardo, *Works and Correspondence*, vol. I, pp. xiii–lxii.

Stanfield, R. (1974), 'Kuhnian Scientific Revolutions and the Keynesian Revolution', *Journal of Economic Issues*, 8, pp. 97–110.

Stark, W. (1959), 'The "Classical Situation" in Political Economy', *Kyklos*, 12, pp. 57–63.

Steuart, J. (1966), *An Inquiry into the Principles of Political Oeconomy* (ed. A. S. Skinner), 2 vols, Oliver & Boyd, Edinburgh.

Stevenson, J. (1974), 'Food Riots in England, 1792–1818', in R. Quinault and J. Stevenson, *Popular Protest and Public Order*, Allen & Unwin, London, pp. 33–74.

Stewart, D. (1811), *Biographical Memoirs of Adam Smith, LL.D., of William Robertson, D.D. and of Thomas Reid, D.D.*, George Ramsay, Edinburgh.

Taylor, W. L. (1965), *Francis Hutcheson and David Hume as Predecessors of Adam Smith*, Duke University Press, Durham, N.C.

Therborn, G. (1976), *Science, Class and Society*, New Left Books, London.

Thompson, E. P. (1971), 'The Moral Economy of the English Crowd in the Eighteenth Century', *Past and Present*, no. 50, pp. 76–136.

Thompson, W. (1824), *An Inquiry into the Principles of the Distribution of Wealth most Conducive to Human Happiness*, Longman and others, London.

Torrens, R. (1808), *The Economists Refuted*, S. A. Oddy, London.

Torrens, R. (1815), *An Essay on the External Corn Trade*, J. Hatchard, London.

Tribe, K. (1973), 'On the Production and Structuring of Scientific Knowledges', *Economy and Society*, 2, pp. 465–78.

Tribe, K. (1976), 'Ground Rent and the Formation of Classical Political Economy: A Theoretical History', unpublished PhD thesis, Cambridge.

Tribe, K. (1977a), 'Economic Property and the Theorisation of Ground Rent', *Economy and Society*, 6, pp. 69–88.

Tribe, K. (1977b), 'The "Histories" of Economic Discourse', *Economy and Society*, 6, pp. 314–44.

Tull, J. (1733) *The Horse-Hoing Husbandry: or, an Essay on the Principles of Tillage and Vegetation*, London.

Tully, J. (1977), 'John Locke's Writings on Property in the Seventeenth Century-Intellectual Context', unpublished PhD thesis, Cambridge.

Tusser, T. (1586), *Five Hundredth Pointes of Good Husbandrie* (corrected and augmented from 1557), London.

Vinogradoff, P. (1892), *Villeinage in England*, Oxford University Press.

Wakefield, D. (1804), *An Essay upon Political Oeconomy*, 2nd ed., London.

Wedderburn, A. (1776), *Essay upon the Question What Proportion of the Produce of Arable Land ought to be paid as Rent to the Landlord?*, Edinburgh.

West, E. (1815), *Essay on the Application of Capital to Land, with Observations Shewing the Impolicy of any Great Restriction of the Importation of Corn*, London.

Worlidge, J. (1675), *Systema Agricultura: the Mystery of Husbandry Discovered*, 2nd ed., London.

Xenophon (1727), *The Science of Good Husbandry: or, the Oeconomics of Xenophon, Showing the Method of Ruling and Ordering a Family, and of Managing a Farm to the Best Advantage*, trans. Bradley, London.

Xenophon, (1897), *The Economist: Works of Xenophon*, vol. III, Pt I, pp. 197–290, Macmillan, London.

Young, A. (1770a), *A Six Months Tour through the North of England*, 4 vols, W. Nicoll, London.

Young, A. (1770b), *A Course of Experimental Husbandry*, 2 vols, J. Dodsley, London.

Young, A. (1770c), *The Farmer's Guide in Hiring and Stocking Farms*, 2 vols, W. Strahan and W. Nicoll, London.

Young, A. (1770d), *Rural Oeconomy: or Essays on the Practical Parts of Husbandry*, T. Becket, London.

Young, A. (1771a), *The Farmer's Kalendar*, Robinson & Roberts, London.

Young, A. (1771b), *The Farmer's Letters to the People of England*, 2 vols, 3rd ed., W. Nicoll, London.

Young, A. (1772), *A Six Weeks Tour, through the Southern Counties of England and Wales*, 3rd ed., W. Nicoll, London.

Young, A. (1788), 'On the Profit of a Farm', *Annals of Agriculture*, 9, pp. 235–44.

Young, A. (1792), *Travels, During the Years 1787, 1788, and 1789. Undertaken more particularily with a View of Ascertaining the Cultivation, Wealth, Resources, and National Prosperity of the Kingdom of France*, 2nd. ed., W. Richardson, London.

Zahar, E. G. (1973), 'Why did Einstein's Programme Supersede Lorentz's?', *British Journal for the Philosophy of Science*, 24, pp. 95–125, 223–62.

Index